Artificial intelligence can be a tremendous time-saver for school lead[...] overlook the best opportunities to use it across our numerous areas o[...] *AI for School Leaders*, Vickie Echols highlights the key conceptual, ethical, and practical challenges in using generative AI to increase our productivity. Deeply informed by Vickie's years of experience as an educator, this book is loaded with specific scenarios, prompts, and cautions for school leaders who want to use AI effectively and responsibly.

> — *Justin Baeder, PhD, Director, The Principal Center, Author and former principal in Seattle, WA Public Schools*

In *AI for School Leaders*, Ms. Echols presents an introduction to artificial intelligence for newcomers and paints a clear picture of the benefits such a tool can provide to school leaders at all levels. Her guide has a variety of useful prompts to assist in everything from improving staff morale to updating operational systems and everything in between. She also takes time to name concerns about overreliance, privacy, and academic integrity; important considerations for every school to be aware of as we find more and more aspects of our work altered by AI. Her ideas and suggestions are grounded in the ISTE Standards and built upon years of experience in education. The practical suggestions found in this book will benefit any educator looking to improve their practice and streamline their workflow.

> — *Brandon Smith, Manager of Computer Science Implementation, Tennessee Department of Education*

Gathering from her 30+ years in education as a teacher and school leader, Vickie intentionally weaves together her expertise and experience with her endless appetite for the power of AI. The result is *AI for School Leaders*, an insightful and practical guide, jam-packed with creative and action-oriented strategies for incorporating AI into your daily routine to support your overall well-being. Vickie's infectious enthusiasm for AI and her authentic care for educators, students, and the field of education at large is palpable. Whether you're a school or district leader or an aspiring teacher leader, let Vickie be your guide in harnessing AI to bolster you and those you care for, both professionally and personally.

> — *Dr. Kathryn Kennedy, Founder of Consult4Ed Group & Wellness for Educators*

Couched in the real need for balance in educators' busy lives, this innovative, ground-breaking, and accessible work offers administrators every AI essential, initial step-by-step instruction, and sophisticated cautions to avoid missteps. All educators will appreciate the 62 practical protocols alongside guiding principles to refine prompts and leverage AI. Echols's encouraging, even joyful, strategies will open closed minds to the power, positivity, creativity, and potential of AI as a tool to benefit students, schools, and communities.

> — *Sherron K. Roberts, EdD, Professor of Language Arts and Literacy Education, The School of Teacher Education, College of Community Innovation & Education, University of Central Florida, Orlando, FL*

Vickie Echols has created a guide for maximizing time by using AI as a beneficial tool in the school setting. This book provides leaders with robust strategies for using AI to enhance day-to-day routines and administrative duties. Additionally, she offers educational leaders tips and tools for safely utilizing AI to create real change in their own school settings. As I read the book, I could envision campus principals implementing these AI tools to reduce mundane tasks, and as a result, spending more time interacting with students and teachers. Principals can use many of the tools and strategies to create an innovative learning culture on their campuses.

> — *Teresa J. Farler, EdD, Assistant Professor, Educational Leadership at Texas A&M University-Commerce, retired Superintendent, Assistant Superintendent for Curriculum and Instruction, and Campus Principal*

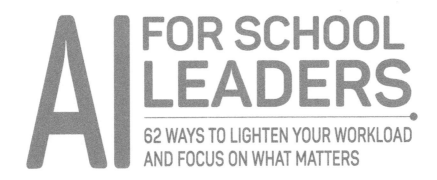

AI FOR SCHOOL LEADERS

62 WAYS TO LIGHTEN YOUR WORKLOAD AND FOCUS ON WHAT MATTERS

VICKIE F. ECHOLS

International Society for Technology in Education

ARLINGTON, VIRGINIA

AI for School Leaders
62 Ways to Lighten Your Workload and Focus on What Matters
Vickie F. Echols

Director of Books and Journals: *Emily Reed*
Senior Acquisitions Editor: *Valerie Witte*
Editor: *Stephanie Argy*
Copy Editor: *Lisa Hein*
Proofreader: *Emily Padgett*
Indexer: *Kento Ikeda*
Book Design and Production: *Kim McGovern*
Cover Design: *Georgia Park*

Library of Congress Cataloging-in-Publication Data

Names: Echols, Vickie F., author.
Title: AI for school leaders : 62 ways to lighten your workload and focus
  on what matters / Vickie F. Echols.
Other titles: Artificial intelligence for school leaders
Identifiers: LCCN 2024013431 (print) | LCCN 2024013432 (ebook) | ISBN
  9798888370322 (paperback) | ISBN 9798888370308 (epub) | ISBN 9798888370315 (pdf)
Subjects: LCSH: Artificial intelligence—Educational applications. |
  Educational leadership. | School management and organization.
Classification: LCC LB1028.43 .E24 2024 (print) | LCC LB1028.43 (ebook) |
  DDC 370.0285/63—dc23/eng/20240514
LC record available at https://lccn.loc.gov/2024013431
LC ebook record available at https://lccn.loc.gov/2024013432

First Edition
ISBN: 979-8-88837-032-2

Ebook version available
ISBN EPUB: 979-8-88837-030-8
ISBN PDF: 979-8-88837-031-5

Printed in the United States of America

Cover Art: © 2024
Inside Art: © 2024

ISTE® is a registered trademark of the International Society for Technology in Education.

About ISTE

The International Society for Technology in Education (ISTE) is home to a passionate community of global educators who believe in the power of technology to transform teaching and learning, accelerate innovation and solve tough problems in education.

ISTE inspires the creation of solutions and connections that improve opportunities for all learners by delivering: practical guidance, evidence-based professional learning, virtual networks, thought-provoking events and the ISTE Standards. ISTE is also the leading publisher of books focused on technology in education. For more information or to become an ISTE member, visit iste.org. Subscribe to ISTE's YouTube channel and connect with ISTE on X, Facebook and LinkedIn.

Related ISTE Titles

How to Teach AI: Weaving Strategies and Activities into Any Content Area
by Rachelle Dené Poth (2024)

Tech for Teacher Wellness: Strategies for a Healthy Life and Sustainable Career
by Meredith Masar Boullion (2023)

AI in the Classroom: Strategies and Activities to Enrich Student Learning
by Nancye Blair Black (2023) (jump start guide)

Understanding Student Data Privacy: A Guide for Educators
by Laurel Aguilar-Kirchhoff (2024) (jump start guide)

To see all books available from ISTE, please visit iste.org/books.

About the Author

 Meet **Vickie Echols**, a professional consultant, dedicated educator, and certified coach. If her career were a quilt, it would be stitched together with threads representing a variety of colorful roles in the journey of teaching and learning. Vickie served as a K–12 and university teacher in East Texas for many years. She was an elementary principal on three campuses in Longview and Duncanville, Texas. At the district level, she worked as curriculum coordinator, director of an education foundation, and director of communication and grants. After her tenure in public schools, Vickie transitioned into consultancy and coaching, joining the Momentous Institute in Dallas, Texas, where she provided guidance at the intersection of mental health and education. She is currently a school transformation coach for the non-profit group Wellness for Educators. She earned a Bachelor of Arts degree from Texas A&M University and a Masters in Education from James Cook University in Australia. She and her husband currently live in Fairview, Texas, where they are close to family. You can connect with Vickie on LinkedIn and at www.vickieechols.com.

Acknowledgments

ISTE gratefully acknowledges the contributions of the following:

ISTE Standards Reviewers

Meredith Bates, Lisa Blank, Mary Beth Clifton, John Padula, Josh Rayburn, Wanda Scanlon Wagner

Manuscript Reviewers

Ajayi Anwansedo, April Burton, Elizabeth Nye Di Cataldo, Stacy Hawthorne

Dedication

Dedicated to the education pioneers whose passionate commitment and bold innovation propel us forward, shaping a brighter future for generations to come. With heartfelt gratitude to the entire ISTE team, especially Valerie Witte, Senior Acquisitions Editor, Stephanie Argy, Project Editor, and Lisa Hein, Copy Editor. And many thanks to my incredible support system—Brad, Sherron, Robin, Kathryn, Stephanie, Tara, Kelly, Tiffany, Nick, Rachel, Ross, Kristin, Angela, Sandi, Richard, Christine, Bert, Beverly, Perry, Bruce, Ken, Billie-Anne and Betty, my dear mom. Your encouragement is a driving force; you inspire me every day.

Contents

Chapter 4

SUPPORTIVE RELATIONSHIPS AND TRUST 59

Chapter 5

PERSONALIZED PROFESSIONAL LEARNING 85

Chapter 6

DATA MANAGEMENT AND SCHOOL IMPROVEMENT 113

Chapter 7
FAMILY AND COMMUNITY ENGAGEMENT 137

Introduction

"Do you always walk this fast, Ms. Echols?" That question from a colleague has stuck with me over the years as a reminder of the fast-paced life of a school principal. At the time, I did not realize the toll that lifestyle took on my health. But after a few stress-induced ER trips, I started questioning if this pace was sustainable, not just for me, but for all of us in this career. As a school administrator, I knew the importance of making time for myself and my loved ones. But the very efforts required to create a thriving school environment—effective planning, fostering a positive culture, and supporting staff—often came at the expense of my well-being. I really enjoyed serving as a leader, but I had trouble finding the balance. Maintaining work-life balance is essential, but it can be HARD!

I also wanted my staff to find joy in their work, but the unrelenting pressures created a domino effect. Exhausted leaders can struggle to foster a healthy working environment. Many educators are parents juggling dirty dishes, carpools, or diapers before coming to work each morning. Some are new employees trying to figure out how to do their jobs without spending the night at the school. They need time to plan and grade assignments so they don't have to work in the evenings and on weekends. Creating an effective learning community and fostering a healthy culture is important. But navigating the efforts to pull this off takes a great deal of time and energy. It can also be HARD.

Apparently, I am not alone. Our country is facing a burnout crisis for school administrators, which could prove disastrous for public schools nationwide (DeMatthews, 2021). This crisis for school administrators seriously threatens the well-being of our schools and the educators who keep them running. This is where innovative solutions like artificial intelligence (AI) can offer a lifeline. I discovered this one afternoon when my husband commented that I should check out ChatGPT, a free AI platform. It intrigued me. The more I played with it, the more I saw its potential to support a healthier way to work. It was impressive. In fact, I was so blown away I decided to write this book. I knew I had to share what I've learned about how AI can help school leaders and their teams.

I wrote the book with school administrators in mind, but many of the ideas can apply to anyone who takes the lead. So, if you are a leader who is wondering how AI can support your work, I hope you find these ideas helpful. With the help of AI, you can finally pump the brakes on tedious work and create a more balanced life. As the title indicates, this book focuses on AI for leaders—but it is also a conversation about finding balance and well-being in the leadership role. I invite you to walk alongside me and discover how AI can help in this journey.

The End of Tedious Work

The overwhelming workload on school principals is a pressing concern and well documented in several research studies. According to Lavigne (2016), principals dedicate about 60% of their time to administrative responsibilities, including budget management, personnel issues, and extensive paperwork. With the ever-growing demands of their role, many school leaders find it challenging to effectively manage their time. This difficulty can lead to increased job stress, a precursor to burnout, as highlighted by Grissom and colleagues (2015). Mahfouz et al. (2020) emphasize how stress not only impairs job performance but also significantly impacts the well-being of school leaders. The question is: Can the integration of machines, particularly in the form of artificial intelligence, offer a viable solution for humans?

Integrating AI into school systems has the potential to significantly reduce the burden of time-intensive administrative tasks. This transition not only streamlines these tasks but also opens opportunities for school leaders to invest more time in valuable human interactions and focus on their own well-being. In his 2023 article "The End of Work," Louis Hyman presents an optimistic view of AI integration. He says AI offers the end of tedious work so we can get on with rewarding work that matters (2023).

A Work-Life Balance with AI

You may be thinking, "I don't have *time* to learn about AI right now." But that is exactly why this book is important. My goal is to demonstrate how learning to use AI can actually give educators the bonus of extra time and a healthier lifestyle.

In the hustle and bustle of life, it is easy to lose sight of what truly counts—your health. Personal wellness often takes a backseat to never-ending to-do lists. However, AI offers a solution to better health by streamlining tasks, increasing efficiency, and ultimately enhancing both your well-being and the campus culture.

In her book *The Mind-Body Connection for Educators: Intentional Movement for Wellness*, Dr. Kathryn Kennedy (2023), founder and executive director of Wellness for Educators, emphasizes the importance of prioritizing well-being to be effective. When teachers are tired, stressed, and overwhelmed, giving students a great learning experience becomes difficult. By prioritizing their own wellness, educators not only enhance their physical, mental, and emotional health but also positively influence their students' outcomes and the broader community.

Everyone benefits when wellness is a regular part of daily routines and the school's culture. So, it is time to explore how AI assistance can contribute to this new reality. The shift can influence not only those you lead and your own personal journey but also the entire campus community.

The ideas presented in this book are just a starting point. Used safely, AI will boost productivity, spark creativity, and ignite curiosity. It's time to shake up the traditional confines of the "way we've always done it." Let AI help you achieve greater productivity and enjoy your job. Or, as Nora Osman (2022) put it, "Let's automate the mundane so we can elevate the humane."

How This Book is Organized

Think of this book as a guide for using AI to tackle some of the challenges in your leadership role. You'll find some very useful information about how this tool applies to your daily responsibilities and ultimately lightens your workload—so you can focus on what matters most.

I divide the information into seven chapters that distill key ideas, presenting them in a concise and practical manner. I encourage you to read through all the examples of prompts, or at least skim through them. You will find many interesting topics that may apply to your work.

Chapter 1: Learn About Generative AI

Chapter 1 provides an overview of the basics; it is your crash course in AI for a school setting. You'll learn the essentials of generative artificial intelligence and why it's transforming education. The focus is on helping school leaders understand the basics and what it means for their schools. You'll meet some big names in generative AI, like ChatGPT, Gemini, and others, which are large language models that can carry on conversations and help with simple or complex tasks. The chapter provides practical tips for using AI platforms, such as how to ask clear and concise questions called prompts. Have your computer handy as you will start learning how to craft an effective prompt for the AI assistant.

Chapter 2: Stay Smart With AI

This chapter delves into the crucial aspects of safe and ethical practices for using AI in a school environment. It outlines six ways to stay smart while using generative AI. The content is not meant to scare anyone away from using AI but rather to encourage cautious and proactive actions. I aim to deepen understanding about the risks of AI while offering six ways to use AI responsibly. These include establishing safety standards, protecting privacy, avoiding over-reliance, analyzing for bias, promoting access for all, and assessing for accuracy. The examples in this chapter offer ways to ensure that AI empowers learning while safeguarding students, staff, and the educational mission itself. By understanding these guidelines, educators can use AI safely and mentor others to do the same.

Chapters 3 through 7 offer more than 60 practical topics or use-cases. These chapters are organized into the five themes related to effective school leadership. Selected topics draw from research conducted by the Wallace Foundation (Grissom et al., 2013) on the impact principals have on students and schools. You will also find a correlation to the ISTE Education Leader Standards, which provide the competencies for learning, teaching, and leading with technology. The standards are a comprehensive road map for the effective use of technology in schools worldwide.

Chapter 3: Collaborative Decision-Making

Learn how the AI assistant can assist with collaboration. You will be able to identify problems, develop creative solutions, and analyze and curate different perspectives. This will lead to more inclusive and effective decision-making.

Chapter 4: Supportive Relationships and Trust

Discover how AI can help improve communication and create stronger connections. Efforts to build trust and promote wellness can help you create a healthier school culture for students, teachers, and families.

Chapter 5: Personalized Professional Learning

Learn how AI can serve as your own professional learning coach. Get guidance on strategies, instructional practices, and professional growth opportunities. It can recommend relevant resources and best practices. Use the AI tutor to inform yourself about the newest teaching methods and educational trends.

Chapter 6: Data Management and School Improvement

Learn how to use AI to analyze school data or identify areas for improvement. Let an AI tool generate recommendations that make sense of complex data sets. Write prompts that address routines, design procedures, summarize reports, or help improve the interview process.

Chapter 7: Family and Community Engagement

Learn what AI can do to develop strategies for effective parent and community engagement. An AI assistant can help build stronger partnerships and organize community events. It can also provide guidance on addressing diverse cultural backgrounds. These solutions can help foster inclusivity, engagement, and well-being for all.

Structured Patterns

Chapters 2 through 7 are structured with a predictable pattern: each topic covers a problem, its solution, and an example of a prompt to use with AI. Some topics also discuss acceleration and cautionary aspects.

The Problem introduces a challenge commonly faced by school leaders.

A Solution offers a description of how the problem could be solved using an AI platform.

An Example includes an AI-based prompt ready for you to plug into your favorite chatbot. The prompt demonstrates one way to practically address the problem. The prompts will appear in a slightly grayed box such as this:

 This is how a prompt will appear in the book. Simply copy the text into the prompt box (or the place where you tell the AI what to do) and tweak the wording of the prompt to fit your specific situation.

Acceleration offers additional dynamic prompts that identify opportunities to explore the topic further and approach solutions in new ways.

A Caution provides reminders of potential pitfalls or sensitive areas related to the specific topic.

Consider the information from these chapters as a spark to ignite your creativity. You will find many unique ways to use AI to enhance your work. Read it straight through, or skip around and choose a chapter or topic you would like to read first.

Self and Group Reflection Questions

At the end of each of the chapters 2 through 7, you'll find questions designed to deepen understanding through reflection and conversation. The questions encourage deep introspection and assist you and your team in applying the concepts to your work on a campus. Consider the conversations as a starting point to think about how AI impacts your school and classrooms. Teachers can open up about challenges and solutions with these icebreaker questions. The questions are open-ended, so there are no right or wrong answers. Instead, they offer a chance to process new ideas and create a shared understanding.

I hope the questions provoke a healthy dialogue and lead to safely integrating AI into your school setting in practical ways. Rich conversations with your colleagues can lead to valuable insights and maybe even a few chuckles along the way.

Authorship

I suspect you may be wondering if I used AI as I wrote this book. Of course I did. AI was used—along with other tools—to help prepare and revise many ideas. But rest assured I wrote, edited, and revised it myself along with a wonderful team of smart and invaluable human beings for whom I am most grateful.

I used several AI platforms, mainly my favorites: OpenAI's ChatGPT, Anthropic's Claude, and Google's Gemini (formerly Bard). And I have to admit, I really enjoy using them. I just wish the chatty machines had been around years ago when I used to burn the midnight oil after a long day on campus.

Connections to the ISTE Standards

The ISTE (International Society for Technology in Education) Education Leader Standards provide a framework for effective leadership in integrating technology and digital learning in educational settings. As educational leaders explore integrating AI into their schools, keeping these standards at the forefront is crucial.

The Education Leader Standards are organized into the following five key areas:

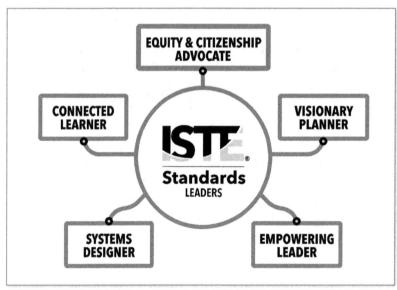

FIGURE I.1 ISTE Standards for Education Leaders.

3.1 Equity and Citizenship Advocate. Ensuring equitable access to technology and digital resources for all students and promoting digital citizenship.

3.2 Visionary Planner. Engaging in strategic planning and fostering a shared vision for the effective use of technology in teaching and learning.

3.3 Empowering Leader. Empowering educators and creating opportunities for professional learning and growth related to technology integration.

3.4 Systems Designer. Leading the implementation and management of effective technology systems and infrastructure.

3.5 Connected Learner. Modeling and promoting continuous learning and growth in technology and digital literacy for themselves and others.

This book weaves references to ISTE Education Leader Standards throughout its practical use cases, highlighting their continued importance in the context of AI implementation. By keeping these standards at the forefront, educational leaders gain a roadmap to navigate the complexities of AI integration thoughtfully and responsibly. This approach fosters the development of digital citizenship, promotes equity, and ensures ethical practices.

Additional Resources

This book includes QR codes, which are digital keys that can unlock a sampling of online resources, each designed to help you on your leadership voyage. Also check out the Appendix and Glossary, which are supplementary resources that include a table linking the ISTE Education Leader Standards to specific topics covered and more.

To dive deeper, visit the companion website, which hosts a collection of resources and research mentioned in this book. Here, you'll have access to downloadable materials and updates to support a variety of activities and initiatives: www.vickieechols.com.

Lean In

Thank you for choosing to read this book. I hope you find AI's capabilities as captivating as I do. My goal is twofold: First, to equip you with tools for sustainable productivity and intentional well-being. And second, to inspire you as a leader to champion the discussion of AI's impact on education. The rapid advancements in AI present a unique opportunity. You can help equip schools with dynamic, learner-centered tools that cater to the individual needs of both students and educators. As you lean in and practice using AI, you will hone your skills and become more efficient and effective in your work. And in doing so, I know you'll reap benefits in your personal well-being and campus culture. This book will be your guide in tailoring AI solutions to your specific needs and campus environment.

While the ideas I present are intended for school administrators, anyone in a leadership role can benefit from them. You will be able to harness AI for increased productivity and well-being, not only for yourself but also for your teams. Yes, there are real concerns about AI, but you have the potential to lead the way in using AI for the greater good. Lean in to explore and discover the interesting possibilities that AI unlocks in this new era.

Chapter 1

LEARN ABOUT GENERATIVE AI

I'VE LEARNED A LOT ABOUT how artificial intelligence can affect education. And one thing I am certain of is this: It is too late to stop it now. AI is rapidly changing the way we think and work like never before (Andreessen, 2023). In this chapter I'll cover the essentials to help you get started. There are different types of artificial intelligence out there, but in this book, I'll focus specifically on *generative* AI. Since I'm an educator learning along with you, I've got experts on board to break it all down. In the coming pages, you'll learn all about this exciting form of AI and gain a solid understanding of how it works.

I won't just stop at the basics, though. I'll also explore the potential benefits of generative AI and share some valuable tips to help you kickstart your journey with this incredible technology. By the time you've finished Chapter 1, you'll feel confident and well-equipped to embark on your very own AI adventure. Get ready to unlock new possibilities and see what generative AI can do for you.

Chapter 1 includes the following topics:

1. Understand The Basics of Generative AI

2. Get Started

3. Narrow Your Focus

Understand the Basics

AI technology is not new. It is already deeply integrated into many aspects of our lives, from our smartphones and vacuum cleaners, to entertainment such as games and movies, and even our cars. Basically, AI is a branch of computer science focused on creating machines that can do things humans can do. It is ubiquitous, so it's important to understand the different types available.

Generative AI refers to artificial intelligence that can create original content, including text, audio, video, images, and computer code. It is not like other computer programs. As the name suggests, generative AI generates unique content from learned patterns. In other words, it can innovate on something that already exists.

Delving into AI means stepping into a world of new words. The Basic Glossary in the Appendix offers a general list of common AI vocabulary terms and links to a more comprehensive list. To keep things clear, I'll be using "AI" throughout this book as short-hand for generative AI. But you may also see it referred to as an AI assistant, chatbot, or even a digital wizard (because that's what it often feels like to me).

Do these machines actually learn? Not really. AI machines train on vast resources such as books, articles, images, and other internet content. During the training process, the machines identify patterns. These patterns are then used to generate the most probable responses to questions or prompts (Shah, 2023 and Lametti, 2022).

Large language models, or LLMs, are a type of generative AI that works with language. Language models are different from older computer programs, which follow only specific instructions. These AI models are supersized, packing thousands or even millions more parameters than the language models from 10 years ago (Toner, 2023).

Generative AI is a relatively new development among the different types of AI technology. It gained prominence with the introduction of ChatGPT during the 2022–2023 school year. Many other models have emerged, such as Google's Gemini, Anthropic's Claude, Microsoft's Bing Chat, and Amazon's Bedrock to name a few. What sets these AI tools apart is their lightning-fast response times, typically less than a second, making it feel like a real-time conversation (Gratas, 2023).

When you use generative AI, it can comprehend, respond, and discuss with you. The AI chatbot can answer questions, participate in conversations, and even tell dad jokes if you like. Large language models have impressive capabilities. However, their limitations come from the quality and diversity of the data on which they are trained. The skills and knowledge of the person who prompts them also play a major role (ISTE, 2023).

You don't need to be an expert to use AI, but having a fundamental grasp of these technologies can empower you to use the new tools wisely. Misunderstandings about AI and machine learning come from not knowing how they work. With a basic understanding, you can use these new technologies more effectively and ethically in a school setting. As AI continues to evolve, it will only become more powerful and versatile. It has the potential to enrich our experiences and interactions with others. For a deeper understanding of how AI operates, consider exploring the Glossary and short guides in the Appendix.

In today's educational landscape, a powerful synergy is emerging between educators and AI. This synergy is captured in the following Venn diagram. We can foster a more effective learning environment by exploring the key areas where human expertise and machine intelligence intersect. While AI excels in data analysis or rapid information processing, educators remain irreplaceable in areas like social-emotional intelligence and ethical decision-making. By understanding this interplay of strengths, we can unlock the full potential of AI to empower educators and ultimately enhance student success.

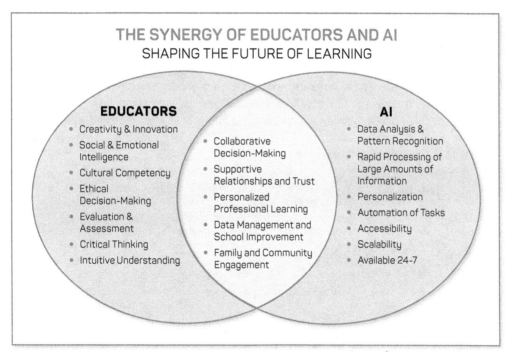

FIGURE 1.1 Educators and AI: A Powerful Partnership.

Get Started: Engineering and Experimenting

Grab your computer, and if you haven't already done so, set up an account in an AI platform. This will enable you to try out the prompts in the book for yourself. The prompts and suggestions discussed in this book are applicable to all generative AI platforms, but the quality and consistency of the responses will vary depending on what you choose to use.

Compare AI Platforms

At the time of publishing, the top generative AI models include OpenAI's ChatGPT, Microsoft Copilot, Anthropic's Claude, Google Gemini, Stable Diffusion, and many others. While I don't endorse any particular one, I recommend trying several platforms and using them to compare answers to your prompt.

- AI platforms may use different language models and algorithms, which can impact the quality and style of the responses. Familiarizing yourself with each model and how they respond can help you decide which platform to use with which prompt.

- Some AI platforms have usage restrictions, pricing models, or ethical considerations that need to be examined. Some offer image creation or allow you to upload images and discuss them. Evaluating these factors can help you make an informed decision about which platform aligns best with your budget and needs.

TABLE 1.1. Examples of AI Platforms

TOOL (Name and Company)	OVERVIEW	COST
ChatGPT-4 *OpenAI*	Text-based AI chatbot; generates text, code, and images. Phone app available	Freemium model with optional paid plans
DALL·E 3 *OpenAI*	Text-to-image AI model; generates images	Paid plans
Claude *Anthropic*	Text-based AI assistant	Freemium model with optional paid plans
Gemini *Google*	Text-based AI chatbot; generates text and images. Includes web search results from a Google Search Engine	Freemium model with optional paid plans
Copilot *Microsoft*	Text-based AI chatbot; generates text, code, and images. Includes web search results from Bing Search	Freemium model with optional paid plans

*These platforms were available at the time of publishing and may have changed. Check for updates at the book's companion site.

Table 1.1 provides a basic overview of some popular AI tools and models offered at the time of publishing. The field of generative AI is rapidly evolving, with new models and platforms emerging weekly. This information may change as new products launch and existing ones are updated. A wiki page published by u-data7 entitled "AI Tools Landscape" (n.d.) provides a more comprehensive overview of various artificial intelligence (AI) tools and resources available. It can offer a starting point for research, learning, and integration into multiple projects or workflows.

Staying informed about the latest developments can help you take advantage of the most advanced and capable AI assistants available. Ultimately, the best AI assistant for you will depend on your specific needs and preferences at the time.

Sign Up for an Account

You typically need to sign up for an account to access and use AI platforms like ChatGPT and others. The sign-up process usually involves providing basic personal information such as your name, email address, and a secure password. Additionally, you'll need to agree to the platform's terms and conditions, which outline the rules and guidelines for using the service. While AI platforms offer exciting possibilities, it's crucial to approach them with caution and awareness. Here are a few important points to consider when signing up for an AI platform account:

Privacy and Data Handling. Review the privacy policy and understand how the platform will handle and use your personal data. Some AI platforms may collect and store your conversations or generated content for training and improving their models.

Terms of Service. It's easy to gloss over this, but take a minute to read the terms of service before agreeing to them. These terms outline your rights and responsibilities, as well as the platform's limitations and disclaimers.

Account Security. Choose a strong and unique password for your account and consider enabling two-factor authentication (2FA) if available. This adds an extra layer of security to your account.

Age Restrictions. Some AI platforms may have age restrictions, typically requiring users to be at least 13 or 18 years old, depending on the platform's policies and local laws.

Responsible Use. AI platforms are powerful tools, and using them responsibly and ethically is essential.

Engineer a Prompt

One of the most important skills to learn is how to start a conversation with an effective prompt. If you are new to using an AI chatbot, it can be helpful to start with simple prompts, such as those in the upcoming exercise. It may take a few attempts to get what you need, but think of the interaction as a conversation. Don't get discouraged; just keep experimenting, and you will eventually find what works best for you. With a little practice, you'll see how AI can be a valuable (and friendly) tool for learning new skills—including how to use an AI assistant.

A *prompt* is a question or a statement telling the chatbot to create or refine something useful for you. Prompt engineering is the process of crafting a message or question that you type, copy and paste, or speak into the AI platform.

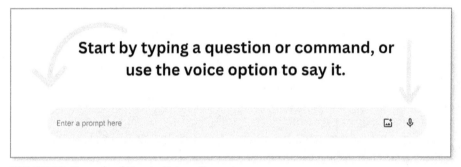

Start by typing a question or command, or use the voice option to say it.

Enter a prompt here

FIGURE 1.2 Example of How to Enter a Prompt.

The more specific you are in your prompt, the better the response you will receive. Details that provide context can influence the output a great deal. Remember, it is a conversation in which you ping ideas back and forth with the machine. It is an iterative process and not hard to learn; just remember to use clear language for the best results. The most effective prompts are specific and concise. If the topic is broad or complex, start small and limit the scope.

After logging in, you can immediately start interacting with the AI assistant by typing a question or a statement. The machine is designed to understand and generate human-like text as if you are having a friendly chat.

Common prompts include asking questions or clarifying content on various topics.

Here are a few prompts to get you started:

> " Brainstorm some ideas for managing my morning routine.

> " What is the definition of the word "pedagogy"?

> " Revise this for me: [insert text].

Experiment with Different Types of Prompts

Learning how to use AI means experimenting with different types of prompts. Here are some popular strategies and frameworks for writing a well-crafted prompt:

FIGURE 1.3 Tips for Using AI.

A. Interactive Conversations

B. Prompt Frameworks

C. Additional Tips for Generating Text

D. Image Generation

A. Interactive Conversations

Interactive conversations are a great way to get to know the AI assistant better. It's also a fun way to learn. The AI assistant communicates with you by exchanging messages back and forth, generating a conversation based on your responses and feedback.

Your first prompt in a chat will start a conversational stream that then builds in complexity with each additional prompt. You ask a question or give it instructions, and after it responds, you follow up with another question or statement. Type your message as if you were talking to a person, and it will try to comprehend what you mean. This interactive aspect is very helpful when the machine gives you something you can't use. You may want to tweak the instructions in the prompt to include additional information. You can keep adding to the conversation within a single stream, so your ideas and questions on the topic are all in one place. Then, when you're ready to change topics, be sure to start a new chat—a new stream—of interaction.

Here's an example of how to participate in an interactive conversation. The following few prompts build a conversation around a specific task for a campus leadership team that is renaming their faculty "lounge." Their goal is to generate a list of new names.

1. TYPE IN YOUR COMMAND OR QUESTION

Suggest some new names for a room at our school building for faculty members to gather for collaboration, professional learning, and socialization. Do not use the word "lounge."

2. USE A DESCRIPTION AND KEYWORDS

Using this description and keywords, generate names for a room on our school campus.

DESCRIPTION: A room for school faculty members to gather.

KEYWORDS: Collaboration, professional learning, socialization

3. ADD SPECIFICITY TO THE PROMPT

The team reviews the output from the chatbot and decides the suggested names need to be more innovative. So, the follow-up prompt below requests more specific details. The AI assistant will know the author wants more names for the room because the prompt is typed into the same conversational stream.

Suggest 10 more names that reflect our mascot, the hornets.

4. ADD EXAMPLES TO THE PROMPT

Giving the chatbot an example can continue the conversation. Adding examples to your prompt can help communicate a more tailored response. And don't worry about asking for more ideas—you can have as many suggestions as you want.

Suggest three more names that reflect our mascot, the hornets. But this time, combine some of the names you suggested, such as: Buzzing Hive.

Interacting with AI provides a reliable and enjoyable exchange of ideas, offering a calm and collected sounding board for your thoughts.

B. Prompt Frameworks

Prompt frameworks are like blueprints for crafting clear, concise instructions for generative AI. These frameworks provide a structure to organize your prompts. There are several benefits to using them. Clearer prompts lead to more relevant and accurate outputs from the AI. Frameworks save time by providing a structure for crafting effective prompts and ensure your prompts are consistent, leading to predictable results from the AI.

Here are a few popular frameworks and examples to try out:

PRO. This framework breaks down prompts into the elements **P**ersona (who is speaking), **R**equest (what you want the AI to do), and **O**utput (desired format).

PERSONA: You are a teacher of 5th-grade students.

REQUEST: Use a template of a 5E lesson plan to reformat the inserted lesson.

OUTPUT: Write the lesson plan in the new format and offer suggestions for improvement.

[insert lesson plan].

APE. This framework focuses on **A**ction (specific task), **P**urpose (why are you doing this), and **E**xpectation (desired outcome).

ACTION: Provide 15 ways to celebrate 25 educators.

PURPOSE: Give the teachers an authentic sense of appreciation during Teacher Appreciation Week.

EXPECTATIONS: Choose cost-effective ideas that will fit into this budget amount [insert amount, e.g., $100.00]. Align with this theme [insert theme, e.g., spring break].

RTF. This framework uses a simple structure of **R**ole (who), **T**ask (what), and **F**ormat (how).

Act as a school principal. Write a message using the following information. School starts at 8 a.m. The building opens at 7:30 a.m., and students are tardy if they are not in the classroom at 8:10 a.m. Use a friendly and professional tone in the format of an announcement.

C. Additional Tips for Generating Text

1. LIMIT OR EXPAND THE CONTENT

The prompt can limit or expand the number of words, paragraphs, characters, or letters of the alphabet. Try the prompt below, which specifies that the beginning of each word is the same. You'll get something in a matter of seconds, such as, "Students, staff, and supplies successfully surfaced for the start of school season." Now that is amazing.

 Write a sentence about going back to school and make every word begin with the letter "S."

2. CONVERT THE POINT OF VIEW OR CHANGE THE PRONOUNS

This tip can come in handy when writing many personal recommendation letters and thank-you notes.

 Convert this text from second-person to third-person point of view: "Brad, your work on the plans for the school playground was outstanding. You coordinated a team to accomplish the task on time and under budget."

3. RESPOND WITH A TABLE RATHER THAN SENTENCES

AI can process and categorize information into organized tables or lists. Using the term "tabulate" in the prompt will direct the chatbot to identify key information and present it clearly and concisely. Some AI models—such as Gemini by Google—offer the option to convert and export the response into a spreadsheet or a document.

 Tabulate the performance of our school's sports teams with the following information for each sport: Basketball, won 5, lost 2, 35 athletes. Soccer, won 4, lost 3, 20 athletes. Volleyball, won 6, lost 0, 15 athletes. Include a win-loss record.

4. TRANSLATION MODE

An AI assistant can translate text into many different languages, which can be useful for communication.

 Translate this from English into Spanish: "I am cool with AI."

It is important to verify the translation with other sources or an expert to ensure accuracy.

D. Image Generation

Have you ever wished you had a tool that could generate unique images based on just a description? Generative AI is making this a reality, and it has the potential to be a game-changer for school leaders. AI systems can create custom visuals from text prompts, allowing leaders to produce flyers, presentations, and social media content that perfectly captures their message. The following table shows a few examples of what is available at the time of publishing.

TABLE 1.2. Sampling of AI Image Generators

PLATFORM	DESCRIPTION
CANVA Exhausted Principal Enthusiastic Principal	A popular no-code graphic design platform that also offers AI image generation capabilities. It uses an AI text-to-image generator that allows users to create custom images and videos with simple text prompts. The first set of images were created with the following prompt: *Generate an exhausted female school principal at her desk.* And then there's this: *Generate an enthusiastic female school principal at her desk using AI to clear the paperwork.*
IMAGE CREATOR *from Microsoft Designer (formerly Bing Image Creator)*	A user-friendly platform that excels at generating high-quality images in various styles. It's particularly good for beginners due to its straightforward interface.
DALL·E 3 *by OpenAI*	A pioneer in AI image generation known for its ability to create incredibly realistic and creative visuals. While access can be limited, it offers a free tier with credits.
ImageFX *by Google*	Another excellent option for beginners. It provides a free and easy-to-use interface for generating creative and fun images based on your descriptions.

How Generative AI Works

Priten Shah, education entrepreneur

Generative AI, the type of AI currently making significant impacts in education, is designed to create new, original content by learning patterns from data fed into it. These models are capable of operating in various forms, including text, images, videos, and music. Although there are numerous methods for training these models, the fundamental process for creating them generally follows this pattern:

Data Preprocessing. Raw data must be cleaned and structured before being utilized for training AI models. Similar to meticulously preparing ingredients before cooking, this process involves eliminating errors, standardizing formats, and isolating relevant information.

Training Phase. In this phase, the AI analyzes vast amounts of data, learning patterns that emerge from the dataset and integrating those patterns into its algorithm. It generalizes the patterns, sequences, and correlations to create a framework for possible new content. For instance, it might learn to associate the word "ice" with both "cream" and "water," based on the likelihood of these words appearing together.

Generation Phase. Once trained, the AI employs its acquired patterns to generate new content. For example, after analyzing thousands of essays, it could produce an original essay on a specified topic. The novel content generated reflects the training data's qualities and characteristics.

Feedback Loop. The learning process continues beyond the initial training. Generative AI receives feedback on the accuracy, relevance, and quality of its outputs as it produces content. This feedback fine-tunes the model, incrementally improving its performance.

Feedback can come from various sources and be used in different ways. For instance, Generative Adversarial Networks (GANs) consist of two competing models: One generates new data, while the other evaluates its authenticity. This rivalry enhances both models, facilitating the generation of high-quality content. Alternatively, some models are trained through human reinforcement learning, where humans assess the outputs and guide the model on which content is preferable.

Furthermore, these models can be integrated with a wide array of software and applications, significantly extending their capabilities. For example, many models are now coupled with search engines, providing them access to external sources that can inform their responses. This feature allows the model to incorporate information not included in its initial dataset without necessitating a complete retraining.

While the processes involved in training and developing these systems are more complex than described here, several key points are particularly relevant for those working in education:

Since AI learns from existing data, it may unintentionally propagate biases present within that data. This underscores the importance of the initial dataset's quality and the training methodologies to mitigate these biases.

These models aim not merely to replicate the dataset but to generate new content based on it. Thus, the outputs are unique and resemble new human-generated content.

Although these models, especially those trained on extensive datasets, may appear to think or recall information, they actually produce content based on identified patterns rather than factual accuracy. Therefore, despite training and integration with knowledge sources like search engines, models are still prone to generating plausible but incorrect information, a phenomenon often referred to as hallucinations.

Narrow Your Focus

Now that you have a basic grasp of how AI works, you are ready to explore how AI can support your work as a leader. Experiment with different types of prompts, and you'll find what works best for you and your specific needs.

The next few chapters will help you get the most out of your AI assistant and use it to its full potential. However, I encourage you to narrow your focus to a few key areas. A targeted approach can help reduce information overload. It may take a few attempts to get what you need. Don't get discouraged; just keep experimenting, and you will eventually find what works best for you to transform the way you lead and live.

Chapter 2

STAY SMART WITH AI

USING GENERATIVE AI IS MUCH LIKE switching from a handsaw to a power saw. The differences in speed and what you can accomplish are amazing. But you also must be super cautious and smart with how you use it. Just as you would not casually operate a power saw without some basic knowledge, you shouldn't use AI without understanding its potential impact. When operating a power saw, you would read the manual and take other safety precautions. It is no different with AI. You have to practice many safety measures. Both tools, if misused, can lead to serious consequences.

According to the famous basketball player Kareem Abdul-Jabbar (2023), "A tool is still a tool, whether it's a stick being used by chimps to fish for termites to eat, or an AI-driven supercomputer that powers a continent. What we do with our tools depends on our creativity, morals, and ability to reason. It will require all three of those qualities to properly and safely move forward with AI" (Abdul-Jabbar, 2023).

Scholars such as Eugene Volokh from UCLA echo these points. They are exploring the accountability aspects of AI-generated content and stress the necessity of clear ethical policies and guidelines. Such standards are crucial for responsible and ethical AI usage (Verma & Oremus, 2023). The integration of AI in educational settings also demands a comprehensive strategy, as noted by Helmore (2023). This calls for continuous dialogue, appropriate regulation, and responsible deployment of these advanced tools.

According to authors Mike Ribble and Marty Park (2019), a comprehensive plan is essential not just for preparing for these opportunities but also for fully leveraging them. Leaders should collaborate with technology experts and a leadership team on campus to ensure there is adequate support and infrastructure. This collaboration will make the technology more effective and accessible for students and adults who use it.

In this chapter, we explore the limitations, concerns, and safety issues associated with using generative AI. As you study the challenges of using AI, consider these six ways to help you stay smart with AI.

FIGURE 2.1 Six Steps to Stay Smart with AI.

1. Establish Safety Standards

THE PROBLEM

Debating the Digital Dilemma

Generative AI in education has sparked more safety research and discussions than ever before. Schools are responding in very different ways, highlighting a variety of perspectives. Some are banning AI in classrooms due to safety concerns, while others allow it with guardrails of responsibility. The potential for AI to improve education is immense, but the safety risks are just as significant. Like any interaction with technology, leaders worry about data breaches and unauthorized access, which could expose sensitive information. These safety vulnerabilities present challenges. And if we don't address them, it could affect privacy, security, and trust in AI's role in education.

THE SOLUTION

Responsible Integration

When Google Apps for Education was introduced as a free tool for schools, I remember an understandable concern about its integration into schools. From 2012 to 2017, Google evolved from a novel option to the backbone of educational infrastructure, marking a transformative era in education (Sabbatini, 2017). This shift wasn't just about adopting new tools; it was about navigating the complex landscape of digital safety. I was a Google evangelist—so excited to launch these tools. However, our journey taught us the importance of a strategic approach to technology, focusing on safeguarding student data and ensuring a secure learning environment. Embracing the new AI tools with a plan will prove that with a focus on security, it's possible to harness the potential of new technologies while maintaining the trust and safety of our school communities.

A Strong Infrastructure

School leaders need to work in partnership with their school's IT specialists to responsibly use AI. These tech-savvy gatekeepers keep the campus technology secure to make sure everyone is safe, so include them at the very beginning. The framework has firewalls, hard passwords, and data encryption. Together, they conjure up a digital barrier, which works its magic in minimizing the risks of data breaches and unauthorized access. The collaboration between school leaders and IT specialists to create a secure digital barrier reflects the systems design approach advocated by ISTE Standard 3.4, Systems Designer.

An AI Use Policy

Safely integrating AI into schools involves an updated policy for using AI. This policy guides AI activities in education by outlining what to do and not to do. An effective policy is important for responsible integration in schools. It helps set up a framework for ethical considerations, privacy regulations, and safety guidelines. The goal is to promote safe, ethical, and effective uses of AI, which align with the school's educational mission. As you update your policy, consider comparing it to an Empowered Use Policy recommended by Scott McLeod (2014). Develop an AI use policy that includes guidelines for ethical considerations and privacy regulations and aligns with the principles of equity and responsible digital citizenship. This example exemplifies ISTE Standard 3.1.d, Cultivate Good Online Behavior, which states, "Cultivate responsible online behavior, including the safe, ethical and legal use of technology."

A Watchful Eye

Remember, technology is ever-evolving, and so are the associated risks. Continuous vigilance is essential. To keep the AI systems secure, they need regular updates and security audits. Verification is one of several ways to ensure safety and ethical standards are in place. Being proactive can help your school find weak spots before they become security problems.

Helpful Partners

When looking for specific platforms, select AI service providers or platforms that prioritize safety and follow established security standards. Vendor compliance is a crucial factor to keep in mind. Leaders at Open AI, the creators of ChatGPT, say they've added safety limits and guardrails to their programming. "There will be other people who don't put some of the safety limits that we put on," the CEO of ChatGPT said in an interview with *The Guardian* (Helmore, 2023). He continued, "Society, I think, has a limited amount of time to figure out how to react to AI, how to regulate, how to handle it." It is worth the time and effort to rigorously vet the vendor's history and product for alignment with your school's safety needs.

In addition to these technical measures, education about how AI tools are used is also vital. Regular staff training by experts about the best practices for AI safety can also help prevent human errors. This type of professional learning promotes digital literacy and encourages ethical decision-making and critical thinking about technology. Providing regular staff training on AI safety aligns with the goal of fostering continuous professional learning and promoting digital literacy as outlined in ISTE Standard 3.5.d, Navigate Continuous Improvement, which states, "Develop the skills needed to lead and navigate change, advance systems and promote a mindset of continuous improvement for how technology can improve learning."

 **AN EXAMPLE**

Use your AI assistant to help create a Responsible Use Policy for AI. Consult experts in referenced articles for guidance by using details from publications and other resources in the prompt.

> Draft a detailed "Responsible Use Policy" that integrates the use of AI in [insert details, e.g., school campus grades K–12]. The policy will establish clear rules and guidelines for language use and monitor activity to ensure the technology is safe and used responsibly with appropriate consequences for misuse.

Instead of starting from scratch, you may just revise your current policy to add information about AI.

> Suggest ways to revise this Responsible Use Policy for technology in our school. Add information about using AI to guide students and staff in learning to use AI responsibly and ethically. [insert copy of current use policy].

2. Protect Data Privacy and Collective Good

THE PROBLEM

Privacy Predicament

Data privacy is of utmost importance in educational settings. Various laws and regulations are in place to safeguard personal information and ensure the safety and security of individuals' data. However, achieving comprehensive security goes beyond mere compliance with laws; it requires the implementation of robust regulations and explicit policies tailored to the specific needs of schools.

Several challenges may arise. First, schools and districts often handle a vast amount of personal information about students, staff, and their families, including academic records, health information, and contact details. Ensuring the privacy and security of this data is paramount, as any breach or misuse could have severe consequences for the individuals involved.

Second, AI systems, particularly generative AI, may inadvertently capture and store sensitive information from user prompts or conversations. Leaders may feel reluctant to put rules around generative AI, concerned that employees will feel untrusted; however, a lenient approach will leave organizations vulnerable to exposure.

 **THE SOLUTION**

Compliance Cornerstone

Schools must implement proactive and stringent measures to prevent data from being retained or misused, even unintentionally. To handle this issue, explore the following steps on how to effectively comply with laws, policies, and guidelines that can ensure data privacy.

The Importance of Compliance

Schools are required to adhere strictly to privacy laws such as the Family Educational Rights and Privacy Act (FERPA). These regulations mandate rigorous steps to safeguard the confidentiality of student records. Compliance with these rules not only ensures legality but also builds trust with students, parents, and staff. Educating and monitoring compliance with privacy laws align with the principles of equity and responsible digital citizenship advocated by ISTE Standard 3.1, Equity and Citizenship Advocate.

Clear Privacy Policies and Guidelines

The privacy policy should be clear and easy to find. It should explain what data will be collected, how it will be stored, and who can see it. This policy for AI use should be included in the broader use policy for all technology use. The policy should cover the concerns of data security, human supervision, and critical thinking in AI-assisted activities. These guidelines help everyone understand privacy rules and commit to following them together. Creating comprehensive policies for AI use aligns with ISTE Standard 3.4, System Designers.

Multiple Layers of Data Security

Securing personal data is not a one-time setup. It is an ongoing process because of the complexities of AI and data analytics. Make sure there are many security layers, such as encryption and secure data storage solutions. Redundancy in security measures is important because it makes it harder for unauthorized people to access information.

Regular Audits and Monitoring

Conducting regular audits for privacy compliance is another crucial step. Audits should go beyond just checking laws; they should also examine how data is accessed in the AI system. By monitoring how AI tools are used, you can identify and address privacy risks early. By focusing on protecting privacy, you're reducing risks and using AI responsibly. You are also protecting student and staff information, which can increase trust in AI systems used on your campus. Conducting regular audits aligns with ISTE Standard 3.4, System Designers.

AN EXAMPLE

To illustrate how AI assistance can help address compliance with laws, policies, and guidelines, especially in regard to privacy in educational settings, try this prompt.

> Develop an AI-powered training module for educators and staff. The module will use interactive scenarios to teach the significance of privacy laws such as FERPA. Activities will feature practical simulations to illustrate responsible management of student data. Include elements of gamification to ensure the training is both informative and engaging, maintaining the interest of all participants.

3. Guard Against Over-Reliance on Technology

THE PROBLEM

Dependency Dilemma

I am a fan of science fiction. In some ways, AI feels as if I have my own robot, like R2-D2 or BB-8 droids from the Star Wars saga. It can simplify complex tasks and improve results in minutes. But just as R2-D2 couldn't save the galaxy by itself, AI cannot independently solve all problems or make decisions without human guidance and oversight. It is merely a tool to improve our capabilities, not a replacement for human judgment and expertise. An over-reliance on this technological ally can lead to some serious pitfalls. AI cannot fully grasp the complexities of human interaction. Overreliance can lead to a neglect of the emotional and situational nuances, which humans uniquely understand. While the AI chatbot may seem like a potent lightsaber, remember it won't become a Jedi Master of Creativity on its own.

THE SOLUTION

Synergistic Partnerships

Rather than solely depending on an AI computer program, blend its capabilities with your own intuition—your "Jedi wisdom"—to cocreate effectively. Here are some ways to combine the practicality of AI with the richness of human intellect.

Prioritize Human Interaction in Communication

AI can help us communicate in various ways, especially through email, texting, and social media. But it is important to note these tools cannot replace the human aspects of communication. Handwritten notes and face-to-face conversations still hold incredible value in an educational setting. They convey nuances and emotional subtleties a machine just can't capture. Technology should enhance communication, not supplant it. In a publication on the future of teaching and learning with AI, the authors compare AI technology to riding an electric bicycle, but not to operating a robotic vacuum (Cardona, et al. 2023). With the electric bike, you are in control. The technology helps propel you in ways you couldn't on your own. But with the robotic vacuum, it works on its own and sometimes ends up sucking the socks left under the bed. The idea that technology should enhance communication, not replace it, aligns with the principles of equity and promoting digital citizenship advocated by ISTE Standard 3.1, Equity and Citizenship Advocate.

Remember, AI is Just a Machine

When working with an AI language model, it can feel as if you are conversing with a human, especially when it uses kind words, such as "please" and "thank you," or says "I'm sorry." Experts caution against thinking of AI models as humans. "No, they haven't decided to teach themselves anything, they don't love you back, and they still are not even a little bit sentient." The models are machines and not intelligent agents (Marcus and Luccioni, 2023). To maintain a good perspective about using AI, it is important to understand exactly how it works.

Critical Thinking and Expertise Are Irreplaceable

While it might seem easy to simply copy, paste, and publish a response from an AI chatbot, verifying its suggestions is essential and requires both time and critical thinking. It's important to cross-check the information with other credible sources to ensure accuracy. Understanding how and when to use AI is key to minimizing errors. The tool is adept at analyzing data and offering recommendations, but human insight and expertise are crucial for interpreting, validating, or challenging these outcomes. Maintaining this equilibrium is vital to ensure AI remains a helpful aid rather than an unverified source of authority. Overdependence on technology can result in errors, so a balanced approach is necessary.

Conversations Are Critical

School leaders must start and sustain discussions about AI in schools. Conversations are critical. A focus on safety and ethics should spark constructive discussions but not lead to fear. We need more discussion about how to use AI with school faculty and with children instead of judging it. Instead of debating AI use, I urge you to engage in informed conversations on how to leverage these tools in schools.

As AI becomes more available, educators need to work with AI companies to help improve the tool. Many companies are willing to work with teachers to solve problems and get their input. It's smart to take a pause in using AI with students until the school staff are comfortable. But do not stop trying to understand how it works. Teachers must take the lead in finding ways to use AI tools in the classroom. Conversations will help. The importance of initiating and sustaining discussions about AI aligns with the principles of visionary planning and stakeholder engagement advocated by ISTE Standard 3.2, Visionary Planner.

 AN EXAMPLE

The concept of "Synergistic Partnerships" between human intellect and AI in a school is both innovative and timely. Here is a way to illustrate this concept effectively. Host workshops with simulated scenarios illustrating how AI tools are used in conjunction with human decision-making. These workshops can demonstrate how AI can provide data-driven insights, while educators use their expertise and judgment to make the final decisions.

> Create three real-life scenarios for a school setting. In each scenario, the AI tools are used in conjunction with human decision-making. These will be used in a workshop to demonstrate how AI can provide data-driven insights, while educators use their expertise and judgment to make the final decisions.
>
> List 1) the context, 2) an AI Tool available on our campus (provide name), and 3) a description of the scenario.

4. Analyze for Bias and Ethics

 THE PROBLEM

AI's Promises and Pitfalls

AI has great potential to improve our lives, but humans train these systems. Since people decide what information to include in the training, and they decide how to structure the information, the machines respond with subjectivity and bias. Users must recognize how the limited data and potential for bias can skew an AI's responses. Because biases exist in our society, the chatbots have the potential to amplify them in a harmful and unhealthy way.

Dr. Joy Buolamwini, who calls herself a "poet of code," founded the Algorithmic Justice League. She discussed possible bias on the TED stage (2016) and brought up concerns, particularly in facial recognition and biometrics. Policing, education, and healthcare use these technologies. Her research shows that if the teams building these models lack diversity, the bias can continue and intensify. Non-inclusive teams and skewed data can make algorithms produce unfair and prejudiced results. Her work highlights this as a significant drawback of AI systems. Lack of transparency around how these tools function can impede accountability.

 **THE SOLUTION**

Ethical Endeavors

If we develop AI in a more inclusive and ethical way, we can enjoy its benefits and avoid setbacks to progress and equality. Ongoing collaboration is crucial among tech companies, researchers, policymakers, school leaders, and the public to develop powerful and responsible AI. How can you as a school leader protect against bias? Start by understanding how bias shows up.

Understand AI Limitations

As with any technology, we must use it with great care. AI algorithms, like all algorithms, depend on the data they are given. We must be vigilant to make sure bias is not baked into AI systems (Cardona, et al., 2023). So, it is important to teach everyone, including faculty and students, about the limits and biases of AI. Armed with this knowledge, users can assess AI-generated content with a critical eye. The key is to be aware of its limitations and biases and to integrate human expertise for a more responsible and wise application of AI tools. When human intelligence collaborates with AI, the result is often more ethical, accurate, and impactful. This solution aligns with the principles of equity and digital citizenship advocated by ISTE Standard 3.1, Equity and Citizenship Advocate.

Evaluate AI Tools Thoroughly

Before using AI tools in your school, make sure to test them as you would with any other resource. Check for fairness across gender, race, ability, and other factors. An independent audit can uncover hidden biases. Vetting AI before adoption prevents perpetuating discrimination through automated systems. Take the time to examine tools rather than immediately deploying them.

Require Human Oversight

For any high-stakes decisions driven by AI, make it a requirement to review perspectives. Set up a team of volunteers who can monitor and review decisions with input from other stakeholders. Technology should complement human intelligence rather than replace it. So, let AI help make decisions, but expect your people to always have the final say in important matters. Combine AI's abilities with human judgment and ethics. Schools can use AI safely by being vigilant and careful to protect students from risks. To adopt AI wisely, we need ongoing education, careful tool selection, and human supervision. This idea aligns with the principles of empowering leadership and human intelligence advocated by ISTE Standard 3.3, Empowering Leader.

Provide AI Ethics Training

To stay smart with AI, ensure your campus staff receives AI ethics and bias training. Discuss appropriate use cases and limitations. Teachers need to understand how to use AI-powered resources in the classroom responsibly. Continuous education about responsible AI use helps faculty recognize problems. It also reinforces the value of vigilance for staff and students. Ethics training aligns with the principles of continuous professional learning and responsible technology use advocated by ISTE Standard 3.5, Connected Leader.

 AN EXAMPLE

Analyzing what you have included or excluded from the data you collect may help you uncover biases and anticipate consequences. In this example, the AI assistant helps you analyze the type of data to collect for a specific issue or situation.

 Act as a school leader. Your goal is to collect inclusive and ethical data to help with a specific issue. List examples of data I can collect so that I can better understand this issue and ways to solve it: [insert topic of study, e.g., students are not arriving at school on time].

Let the AI chatbot help you design a training session that focuses on staying smart with AI.

 Design a half-hour training session for educators to enhance their understanding about the capabilities and concerns of AI, specifically [insert details, e.g., analyzing for bias, protecting privacy]. The goal of the session is to empower them to make informed decisions about when and how to integrate AI technology into their teaching practices. Engage participants by using a game or small-group interaction to learn the information.

5. Promote Access for All

THE PROBLEM

The Digital Divide

During my time teaching at a high-poverty elementary school, I saw firsthand how the digital divide can create significant challenges for students. Many of my students didn't have access to computers or the internet at home, and even in the classroom, technology resources were limited. As AI becomes more prevalent in education, we must address this issue of unequal access head-on. If students from under-resourced communities can't utilize AI tools, they risk falling behind their peers who do have access to these powerful technologies.

There are several obstacles that can prevent schools from fully integrating AI, including budget constraints, lack of teacher training, and skepticism about adopting new technologies. But the achievement gap could widen even further if we don't overcome these hurdles. Unequal access to AI isn't just an educational issue—it's a civil rights issue. Students who don't have the same technological opportunities may face barriers to future success. The immense potential of AI in education can only be fully realized if all students, regardless of their backgrounds, can benefit from it.

We cannot allow the transformative power of AI to become a privilege enjoyed only by those with means. Every student deserves access to the tools that will prepare them for the 21st century world and workforce. As AI becomes more integrated into schools, as highlighted by Michael Gaskell (2024) in his article "How School Leaders Can Address the Inequities of the AI Digital Divide," it's going to be up to school leaders to make sure this integration is equitable. This means ensuring all students have access to the technology, training, and support needed to benefit from AI-powered learning experiences.

THE SOLUTION

Bridging the Gap

What if AI could be a force for equity, not a tool for exclusion? To ensure all students thrive in an AI-powered future, our priority must focus on achieving digital equity. This requires not only fair and responsible use of AI in education but also a commitment to continuous improvement in school practices. Let's explore key strategies school leaders can use to prioritize inclusion:

Empowerment and Digital Literacy

Teachers need to become comfortable using AI before granting students access. Equipped with adequate training in digital literacy and informed about AI, teachers can effectively guide students in navigating and harnessing the full potential of AI in their learning journey. This aligns with the principles of empowering leadership and professional agency advocated by ISTE Standard 3.3, Empowering Leader.

Continuous Evaluation and Improvement

Regularly review the impact of AI tools used in your school. Are the tools improving outcomes equitably across student groups? Gather feedback from teachers, students, and families. Find areas to improve and address concerns. Be prepared to refine implementation strategies based on impact evaluations and stakeholder input. Evaluating AI systems helps fix problems and ensures they support all types of learners. This aligns with the principles of systems design and continual improvement advocated by ISTE Standard 3.4, Systems Designer.

Prioritize Partnerships

Working with a mix of people and perspectives is key to bringing out the best in what we do, especially with AI in education. It's all about understanding different needs. Why not team up with organizations like ISTE and others in your local community who can help identify any biases or issues that could affect underserved students? This approach supports active involvement with all stakeholders, as recommended by ISTE Standard 3.2, Visionary Planner, and promotes fairness and digital responsibility, in line with ISTE Standard 3.1, Equity and Citizenship Advocate.

 AN EXAMPLE

This prompt helps you find organizations that support professional learning for educators. The AI assistant can improve your network and broaden your understanding of AI's abilities and limitations.

 Provide a list of organizations, including ISTE, which offer educators a safe community for learning, advocating and gaining information about AI products.

6. Assess for Accuracy

 THE PROBLEM

The Reality Riddle

An issue with AI responses, as with any information found online, is the lack of guarantee for accuracy as a single source (McClennen and Poth, 2022). This can get tricky. It means educators and students must be cautious and critical thinkers when using AI-generated content. This problem can cause the spread of false information and harm educational outcomes. Despite its confident, sophisticated, and authoritative tone, AI tools can provide incorrect information.

 THE SOLUTION

Content Confirmation

To address this challenge, encourage your staff to verify information from reliable sources. This is an essential skill in the age of AI, and it is something to teach and practice. Think of AI's outputs only as a starting point, rather than the final answer. To get better at telling if information is true, try these strategies.

Double-Check Your Facts

I have used AI to help me cook my Thanksgiving ham and to plan a vacation, and it worked out great. But when using an AI tool for academic learning, I recommend comparing responses with several platforms and with information from experts. You can find helpful information from articles in databases such as the Education Resources Information Center (ERIC), and professional communities like ISTE or ASCD. This aligns with the principles of staying informed and utilizing resources effectively advocated by ISTE Standard 3.5, Connected Leader.

Compare Notes

Many AI tools that aim to boost student engagement are becoming available to schools. It's essential, however, to do your homework before diving in. Prior to using a new program that promises to enhance student engagement, make sure you learn the facts. Research the program with your AI assistant and conduct an internet search of experts on the topic. These actions emphasize the need to compare new programs promising to enhance student engagement and align with the principles of visionary planning and informed decision-making advocated by ISTE Standard 3.2, Visionary Planner.

Keep the Context in Mind

AI tools work well for many situations, but schools have unique needs. For instance, an AI tool advertised as working well in a suburban high school may not yield the same results in an inner-city elementary campus. Keep your school community's unique needs and context in mind when evaluating the suitability of any AI tool.

 AN EXAMPLE

This example begins with a prompt to ask about effective programs for academic success. It then builds on the first response to ask for additional information in subsequent prompts. For this prompt, I used Google's Gemini, which sometimes provides links for further research.

 List educational programs that use generative AI and claim to increase student engagement in creative writing through technology.

Next, ensure the program meets ISTE standards, as ISTE provides evidence-based perspectives for confirming or challenging technology programs. Try the following prompt to verify how the program aligns with these standards.

 This educational program claims to increase student engagement through technology: [Insert name of the program, e.g. "Writesonic"]. Analyze this program and compare it to the standards for technology reported by the International Society for Technology in Education (ISTE).

Discussion Questions: Stay Smart with AI

While it is true AI can make mistakes, its advantages are significantly greater. The synergy of AI and human supervision forms a robust partnership. This chapter offers insights into staying smart with AI. As you navigate this new tool with these safeguards in mind, AI will become a valuable and ethically responsible component for shaping how we learn in schools.

Use these questions with your team to discuss how to stay smart with AI tools in a school setting.

1. How do we ensure the accuracy of AI-generated outcomes when using AI tools on our school campus? What steps or strategies do we use to confirm and verify the results?

2. What safety measures do we have on our campus for using AI tools in education? How do we prioritize the well-being and privacy of students and stakeholders?

3. How do we navigate the ethical considerations that arise from using AI tools in our school?

4. How can we keep up with the changing ethical guidelines and best practices for using AI?

5. How can we educate and include stakeholders, such as parents and the community, about AI tool safety and accuracy in schools? How do you foster trust and address any concerns or misconceptions?

6. How do we track and test the safety and accuracy of AI tools over time? How do we ensure continuous improvement and change as needed?

7. How can we involve students in discussions and the decision-making process related to the safety, ethics, and accuracy of AI tools? How do you empower them to voice their opinions and contribute to shaping AI practices in the school?

Chapter 3

COLLABORATIVE DECISION-MAKING

AS LEADERS, YOU FACE some serious challenges in today's rapidly changing landscape. You must stay agile while keeping a steady hand on the helm. It can get overwhelming—enough to make anyone feel adrift. I know that isolated feeling all too well.

I remember the first time I stepped into the role of a campus principal. The adage "lonely at the top" was not far off. I struggled at first, trying to make decisions that would have a positive impact while juggling so many priorities. I eventually realized the key to success was engaging others in collaboration. By involving a trusted team in decision-making and leveraging the expertise of each member, I could chart the best path forward. What I didn't have at the time was a tool like AI, which can also be a reliable partner in collaborative decision-making.

This chapter will chart how you can use AI to make decisions as a team. The examples align with ISTE Standard 3.2, Visionary Planner, and Standard 3.3, Empowering Leaders. Working collaboratively is often the best way to experience a culture that allows exploration and experimentation, which can lead to better decision-making. The environment can help employees feel more engaged and build stronger relationships within the team. The result is a more innovative and creative faculty, and a more just and equitable place to work (DeWitt, 2016).

Connection to the ISTE Standards for Leaders

3.2 Visionary Planner
Leaders engage others in establishing a vision, strategic plan and ongoing evaluation cycle for transforming learning with technology.

3.2.a Engage education stakeholders in developing and adopting a shared vision for using technology to improve student success, informed by the learning sciences.

3.2.d Communicate effectively with stakeholders to gather input on the plan, celebrate successes and engage in a continuous improvement cycle.

3.3 Empowering Leader
Leaders create a culture where teachers and learners are empowered to use technology in innovative ways to enrich teaching and learning.

3.3.a Empower educators to exercise professional agency, build teacher leadership skills and pursue personalized professional learning.

3.3.c Inspire a culture of innovation and collaboration that allows the time and space to explore and experiment with digital tools and adoption.

7. Lead with a Collaborative Approach

THE PROBLEM

Conflicting Opinions

Collaboration can result in better decisions, but it can also be a time-consuming and challenging process. Conflicts can also come up during discussions, leading to frustration. The added tension can stall the work. Some people are just more assertive than others, leading to domination and power struggles. It can get complicated. Without intentional training and practice, collaborative decision-making is hard to pull off.

THE SOLUTION

A Collaborative Resolution

Looking back on my early days as an administrator, I remember how conflict seemed like a headache to avoid. I saw friction as something that made our work challenging and stressful. Cooper and Murphy (2016) have a different take on this. They say that a little conflict isn't the end of the world. In fact, it could be just what we need to get to some really great results. How I wish I'd had this nugget of wisdom in my toolbox back then.

I also wonder how things would have worked with an AI assistant in the mix. It could have helped to establish norms, foster a culture of respect, and guide us in leveraging conflict to enhance our skills. This could have alleviated the stress associated with conflict and transformed it into a powerful tool for team development and personal growth. The support of AI in this journey could have made a significant difference, smoothing the path to more effective collaboration and a more joyful learning community.

 ## AN EXAMPLE

An open conversation is a proactive way to strengthen the team and improve collaboration. AI-prompted questions can help identify communication barriers and potential biases, fostering a more equitable and collaborative environment. In this example the leader guides their team in a discussion about collaboration skills, focusuing on inclusive practices. They use questions generated from AI to intentionally address conflict resolution skills. After reviewing the suggested questions, critically evaluate them and choose only those that are the most effective for your team.

 You are a school leader who is meeting with a team to discuss and assess their current collaboration skills. Create a list of questions that will help identify communication barriers and potential biases, fostering a more equitable and collaborative environment. The goal is to encourage the team members to talk about their communication norms, conflict resolution skills, and teamwork. The outcome is a proactive session that will strengthen the team and improve collaboration.

This example illustrates ISTE Standard 3.1.c, Model Digital Citizenship, which states, "Model digital citizenship by critically evaluating online resources, engaging in civil discourse online and using digital tools to contribute to positive social change."

 ## ACCELERATION

To help your leadership team continue to improve their collaboration skills, try some of these prompts.

Creating Norms For Communication

Prompt the AI assistant to generate a list of norms to use during meetings. Next, discuss the statements on this list with your leadership team. Decide which ones to keep, delete, combine, or add to your team's list and if there are others to consider.

> Considering our mission to [insert school mission] and our roles as leaders within the school, draft a set of norms that will guide our team's interactions and decision-making. These norms should reflect our commitment to fostering open communication, inclusivity, and effective teamwork.

Analyzing Information

The AI assistant can help with a group discussion by providing ideas to inform decision-making.

> Our school leadership team is studying this issue: [insert an issue, e.g., we have many students in 5th grade missing class]. We are seeking a solution that is fair and effective. What sources of information should we analyze to inform the decision-making process?

Resolving Issues

When disagreements pop up and common ground is hard to find, let the AI assistant step in to help resolve the issue.

> The school's computer lab is a resource used by students from all grade levels. However, there is often disagreement about how the lab should be allocated. For example, some teachers and students want to use the lab to have an open schedule to sign up for research projects, while others want a set schedule for all classes to attend each week. How can we resolve this disagreement in a fair and productive way?

Generating Steps and Solutions

When an emotional issue is on the table, designing the discussion can contribute to a healthier and more productive meeting. Let the AI chatbot suggest steps for finding solutions as a group that may not see eye-to-eye on the issue.

> The leadership team is meeting to discuss the dress code for teachers. There is disagreement among the team members about what constitutes appropriate attire for teachers. Some team members believe teachers should dress conservatively, while others believe teachers should be able to express their personal style through their clothing choices. Suggest steps to use during the meeting and offer possible solutions to the issue for consideration.

8. Cultivate Consensus for a Vision and Mission

 ## THE PROBLEM

Mission Impossible?

Can you recite your campus's mission or vision statement? Despite their importance, teachers, families, and students often find these statements forgettable. Crafting a memorable and concise statement is a daunting task, marked by lengthy discussions and a quest for consensus that feels nearly impossible.

I remember spending a whole day trying to hash out a mission statement with educators that everyone could agree on. I ended up feeling like we didn't really get anywhere. It left me wondering if it was even worth the time and effort. It just goes to show how tough it is to boil down a shared vision into something concise and powerful.

 ## THE SOLUTION

Your Diplomatic Wordsmith

A vision statement and a mission statement are foundational components of an organization's strategic planning. They serve different but complementary purposes. A vision statement sets the direction and aspiration for the future. A mission statement defines the organization's current activities and purpose, guiding its operations and strategic decisions.

Start by including all who are affected by the vision and mission. Cast a wide net through a survey and focus groups to invite a variety of ideas so you'll get a better chance of buy-in. Ask for answers to these questions:

Vision. Imagine our school/company/organization is at its absolute best, 10 years from now. What does it look like? Describe its impact, the environment it fosters, and the kind of people it attracts. What is the feeling you get when you think about this ideal future state?

Mission. Think about the core purpose of our school/company/organization. What unique value do we bring to the world? Who do we serve? How do we make a difference, every single day? If our mission statement could be a rallying cry, what would it be?

Then with a smaller group, conduct a brainstorm session to discuss the feedback. After collecting all these ideas, let AI help condense these thoughts into a menu of options for a vision or mission statement.

 AN EXAMPLE

This prompt can be used to kick-start the process of combining everyone's ideas into examples. Insert all the contributions into the prompt. After AI creates the vision statements, the group can discuss and agree on the best one.

 Summarize the following ideas into 10 concise vision (or insert "mission") statements. Write each statement in a way so that all who read it will be able to recite it and focus their work on achieving it. [Insert content from the participants, examples below]

1. We foster our students' love for learning, encourage them to try new and exciting things, and give them a solid foundation to build on.

2. Our vision is to develop well-rounded, confident, and responsible individuals who aspire to achieve their full potential. We will do this by providing a welcoming, happy, safe, and supportive learning environment in which everyone is equal and all are celebrated.

3. We believe a happy child is a successful one. We are committed to providing a positive, safe, and stimulating environment for children to learn, where all are valued.

4. Our early learning center exists to provide a safe, developmentally inclusive environment for toddlers, preschool, kindergarten, and school-age children.

These examples align with ISTE Standard 3.2.a, Create Shared Vision, which states, "Engage education stakeholders in developing and adopting a shared vision for using technology to improve student success, informed by the learning sciences."

ACCELERATION

Vision or mission statements should be easy for everyone in the organization to remember or recite. This means the statements are short, clear, and to the point. Try directing the AI assistant to keep the response simple, focusing on conveying the core essence in a limited number of words.

> Simplify these statements. Limit the number of words to 10 or less. [insert statements].

How do you get everyone to agree? Consensus and compromise are two different decision-making approaches. Seeking consensus means gaining agreement among all participants. Finding compromises toward the middle ground can also be effective. Your AI assistant can help with protocols for each of these approaches. This prompt will get you started:

> You are working toward consensus or compromise with a team of people seeking to reach agreement on which words best explain their school vision and mission. Create a list of group protocol exercises, such as "Dot Voting," that we may use in this task. Explain how each protocol works.

A CAUTION

Using AI to generate vision or mission statements comes with several obstacles. AI may find it challenging to replicate the depth of understanding and emotional connection required to provide direction and inspire individuals within an organization. If you don't use your teachers' feedback, the AI's suggestions might follow current trends instead of what your school needs. AI is a machine and lacks feelings, emotions, or intuition. Therefore, it may not understand human values as deeply as a statement made by a person. So be sure to tweak the suggestions to spark a statement that sticks.

9. Generate Ideas for a Plan or Project

 THE PROBLEM

Strategic Stagnation

Revamping a school's strategic plan can be a daunting endeavor. One year, when trying to revamp our school's strategic plan for wellness and engagement, I remember hitting a wall with what seemed like the same old ideas. It felt as if we were going in circles, unable to break free from "the way we've always done it." The strategies we were using no longer met our needs. The real challenge was sifting through the vast sea of research and opinions to find fresh, actionable insights that could truly make a difference. We needed something that would not only resonate with our school's unique culture but also energize the team to think outside the box. If only we'd had a tool to help us brainstorm and generate ideas from the experts.

 THE SOLUTION

Collaborative Clarity

AI can become your strategic partner, streamlining research and curating the most relevant resources and innovative strategies tailored to your unique needs. Imagine brainstorming sessions fueled by expert insights, empowering you to explore creative solutions for staff well-being and student engagement.

 AN EXAMPLE

In this scenario, AI compiles resources and strategies for creating a wellness initiative to combat the teacher shortage. While a traditional search engine could serve a similar purpose, the AI platform streamlines the search process, making it more efficient to locate these resources.

> Given the concerning rates of educator burnout and the growing teacher shortages, our campus is actively seeking strategies to enhance well-being and encourage long-term employment among our staff. We seek ideas that address systems, collective initiatives, and individual support. Provide a list with various online published materials—such as blog posts, articles, books, and reports—that provide actionable ideas and insights for crafting a comprehensive wellness plan tailored to the needs of educators. For each recommended resource, specify the type (e.g., book, article, handbook) and include a summary of its contents or key takeaways, if such information is available.

These examples align with ISTE Standard 3.5.a, Stay Current on Innovation in Learning, which states, "Set goals to remain current on emerging technologies for learning, innovations in pedagogy and advancements in the learning sciences."

ACCELERATION

Leverage AI to summarize expert advice. Start by gathering relevant articles, reports, or studies. Next, copy the pertinent sections of these resources and paste them into the AI assistant's prompt window. Request a summary to have AI distill the key insights from the content. Using this approach, you can efficiently extract and use expert advice to get actionable ideas and information.

> I have collected several articles, reports, and studies on [topic] and would like to understand the expert advice contained within them. Below, I have pasted relevant sections from these sources. Summarize the key points and insights. This summary will help me craft content for a newsletter/blog post or facilitate discussions within my team. [Copy/paste key information from the articles, reports and studies into the prompt.]

A CAUTION

As you look through the list of resources offered from the AI tool, you may run into some dead ends. This is partly because AI, like any advanced computational system, can experience what is often referred to as *hallucinations*. These are instances where the AI generates information or conclusions that, while plausible sounding, are not based in factual accuracy or reality. This phenomenon occurs due to the AI's reliance on patterns in the data it has been trained on rather than access to real-time, verified information. It's important to approach AI-generated content with a critical eye, verifying facts independently when accuracy is crucial.

10. Master the Details

THE PROBLEM

Setup Slip-Ups

Meetings are crucial for teamwork, but poorly run ones can be draining. I recall attending a meeting with no prior agenda sent out and none provided at the meeting. There weren't enough chairs, so the meeting started and ran late. As the speaker droned on about random issues, I found myself scrolling through my phone, counting the minutes until it ended. Overlooking details can break the meeting's flow and waste everyone's time. Just as it does in the classroom, disorganization in a staff meeting can lead teachers to lose focus or forget what was discussed.

 THE SOLUTION

Tame the Detail Devil

Here's where AI steps in as a powerful solution. It can help anticipate and address the logistical hurdles that often plague meetings. AI's strength lies in its ability to create checklists that include all the details for setting you up for success. By understanding the purpose of the meeting, AI can craft a clear and concise agenda, prioritizing agenda items and ensuring they all contribute to the desired outcome. It can intelligently sequence topics, allowing for natural transitions and maximizing efficiency. Or use it to design pre-meeting surveys or questionnaires, collecting topics and discussion points from participants beforehand. By automating these tasks, AI can significantly reduce the time and effort required for meeting preparation. This allows you to focus on what truly matters—facilitating engaging discussions and driving successful outcomes.

 AN EXAMPLE

Let's say you're setting up an interactive learning session with a school faculty. This prompt can get your AI thought partner started.

> Create a detailed checklist of the logistics for setting up an interactive learning session with a school faculty. The environment is welcoming and conducive for small groups to discuss, record, and share new learning with the whole group. Include a list of materials needed. Include a list of healthy food options for snacks during the meeting.

These examples align with ISTE Standard 3.5.a, Stay Current on Innovation in Learning, which states, "Set goals to remain current on emerging technologies for learning, innovations in pedagogy and advancements in the learning sciences."

ACCELERATION

Grease the wheels of collaboration by clearly communicating a meeting schedule for the entire year, and try using your new assistant to create the schedule. Use Google's Gemini to quickly export the spreadsheet to your Google Drive.

> Create a meeting schedule in the form of a spreadsheet for the campus leadership team:
>
> Column headers: Date, Location, Time, Topics, Notes
>
> Rows: Dates - [insert dates, e.g., first Monday of each month Aug-May]. Location - [insert room]. Time - [insert start/end].

11. Curate Questions for Dynamic Discussions

THE PROBLEM

Question Quandary

Crafting questions for a discussion group sometimes has me puzzled. It's not as straightforward as it seems. I'm always overly cautious not to unintentionally ruffle feathers. However, there are occasions when my attempts to spark engagement inadvertently have caused the conversation to shut down. The last thing you want is to hear crickets after asking a question. Even if it sounded good on paper, it doesn't always fuel the conversation as you'd hoped. It's crucial to come up with a diverse range of questions, but it's a challenging and time-consuming endeavor without a good tool in hand.

THE SOLUTION

Your Discussion Dynamizer

When it comes to sparking lively discussions, an AI assistant can be a lifesaver. It swiftly crafts questions tailored to support professional growth and keep the conversation flowing. Start with a set of queries designed to foster connections and unity among the group. This not only sets the tone but also helps gauge everyone's mood. Next, provide information in the prompt to ensure the group questions align with the specific topic and purpose of the meeting.

AN EXAMPLE

Try out this prompt for questions with a grade-level team or department.

> Generate reflective prompts and questions for a grade-level/department team to discuss [insert topic, e.g., working as a team]. Begin with a few questions to help the group connect with each other.

These examples align with ISTE Standard 3.5.c, Engage in Reflective Practice, which states, "Use technology to regularly engage in reflective practices that support personal and professional growth." Connected Learner is part of the ISTE Standards for Education Leadership, a section of the ISTE Standards.

ACCELERATION

Try crowdsourcing your group for ideas. Use a survey to invite participants to submit feedback or questions on a specific topic. This combines the best of human creativity with AI's analytical skills. After collecting the comments and questions, use them in this prompt.

> Analyze these comments from questions on the topic of [insert topic, e.g., work-life balance]. Look for trends of popularity, relevance, and sensitivity. Use these statements and questions to generate a new list of questions for small group discussion: [insert responses].

How about using AI to analyze previous discussion topics and participants' responses? The AI can recognize patterns, preferences, and topics that resonate with your group. It can then help you craft new questions aligned with their interests.

> Analyze these questions and the responses from a previous focus group discussion. Generate a list of new discussion questions that build on the ideas and deepen the conversation for the next session.

12. Collaborate on Ideas

 THE PROBLEM

Lost in the Educational Labyrinth

As both a teacher and an administrator, many of my conversations focused on how to best help students. Finding a solution to help students who struggle is not an easy task. Each situation is unique, making it tough to identify what will actually work. The demands of the day can lead to exhaustion, causing a team to fall back on old ineffective methods. Plus, the lack of time makes it hard to research and apply proven strategies.

 THE SOLUTION

Robust Roundtable

It is important to use a collaborative and multi-tiered approach to interventions to meet the different needs of students. An AI assistant can greatly help a support team generate ideas and choose strategies for each case. The AI-generated suggestions serve as a menu of ideas, helping the team build consensus more efficiently. In this way, decision-making becomes more inclusive, taking into account a variety of fresh perspectives.

 AN EXAMPLE

In the example below, the team is meeting to discuss a student who has received a diagnosis of both attention deficit hyperactivity disorder (ADHD) and autism spectrum disorder (ASD). Several challenges have made it difficult for the student to stay focused and complete assignments.

 You are a teacher of students in third grade. List 5 strategies to modify assignments for a student who has a diagnosis for a high-functioning ADHD and ASD. The student is in a class with 22 typical learners, with one teacher and minimal support of additional personnel. Create a list of materials needed for the classroom.

These examples align with ISTE Standard 3.3.d, Use Tech to Meet Student Learning Needs, which states, "Support educators in using technology to advance learning that meets the diverse learning, cultural and social-emotional needs of individual students."

 **ACCELERATION**

Use Resources in the Mix

Evidence-based practices are key to successful interventions. Try including (copy/paste) the content from reputable resources in the prompt. Be sure to keep this prompt in the same stream as the former prompt so the AI can build off the original query. Here is an example of how to use an online resource to inform and add suggestions to a brainstorming session.

 Below, I have pasted relevant sections from a reputable resource. Summarize the key points and insights. Review this free resource describing a "Strategic Intervention Model" from Momentous Institute (2019). Provide suggestions gleaned from the information to help our team of educators brainstorm solutions for ways to support the student described in the previous prompt: [Copy/paste content from the resource mentioned above].

Decide if the AI assistant's response needs more or less details because the level of detail in the prompt affects the AI assistant's response. To help the AI tool give better recommendations and share classroom information, teaching approaches, and resources, this tool can give customized suggestions for student learning.

Use Frameworks for Analysis

This prompt helps you guide the conversation around a specific framework. Using a SWOT analysis, your team can approach the situation with a broader understanding of the issues.

 Help our leadership team conduct a SWOT Analysis (Strengths, Weaknesses, Opportunities, Threats). We need to decide how to improve [insert issue, e.g., interventions for disruptive behaviors]. Give us an example of how to identify internal strengths and weaknesses and external opportunities and threats.

 **A CAUTION**

To protect privacy and security, never share sensitive or personal information in the prompt. Avoid adding personal details such as names, email addresses, or any identifying information to the prompt.

13. Write a Team Proposal

 THE PROBLEM

Proposal Predicament

To improve common areas on campus, such as a lackluster library or a boring playground, you need ideas and money. Successful grants or community partnerships can be a solution, but proposals are time-consuming. Crafting a compelling proposal involves attention to content, language, and structure. Going solo may seem tempting, but projects usually thrive on collective support from a team to launch a successful grant.

 THE SOLUTION

Proposal Perfection

Teamwork, enhanced by AI, can elevate your proposal from good to exceptional. AI can help brainstorm compelling ideas and collate the research needed to support them. It can help write compelling stories for an appealing proposal using its amazing language skills.

It can also ensure your proposal follows a professional, easy-to-read format. And it doesn't stop there; it can help with delegation, allowing each team member to contribute their unique skills and expertise. The result? A higher likelihood of securing that much-needed money to fund the new project.

 **AN EXAMPLE**

Use the following prompt to generate custom content for grant proposals. Include details to customize the proposal in alignment with the application. The more specific the prompt, the better the results.

These examples align with ISTE Standard 3.3.c, Inspire a Culture of Innovation, which states, "Inspire a culture of innovation and collaboration that allows the time and space to explore and experiment with digital tools and adoption."

Write a grant proposal and provide compelling content for each of these sections.

Introduction: Clearly describe the problem we are trying to solve and the need for the project [insert notes on problem and need].

Proposed solution: Describe specific changes and how they will address the problem [insert a list of details].

Background: Provide information about the current project and the challenges users face [insert details].

Benefits: Quantify the following benefits of the renovation, [insert details, e.g., the number of students who will benefit]. Quantify the time and money saved and the impact on the school as a whole.

Funding: Explain how the project will be funded [insert details about funding options].

Conclusion: Summarize the key points of the proposal and make a call to action.

 ACCELERATION

Some grants are more comprehensive and require specific key sections. These prompts may help you complete those sections.

Letter of Inquiry Template

 Write a letter of inquiry for a grant proposal using the following information:

Project Name: [insert name]

Annual Budget: [insert amount]

Funding Use: [insert rationale]

Funding Organization: [insert the name of the grantor]

Funding Organization Priorities: [insert the funding priorities of the grantor. These are usually found in the grant proposal]

Organizational Background: Tell Your School's Story

Write the section for a grant proposal telling our school story. Include the following information:

Project Name: [insert name]

School Location: [insert location]

Project Staff Introduction: [insert roles of key leaders who will guide the project, their qualifications, and relevant experiences each bring to the activities planned]

Achievements: [insert details]

Funding Use: [insert rationale]

Statement of Need Template

You are writing a section of a grant proposal called the statement of need. Craft a compelling paragraph describing why the funding organization should grant the award to our school.

Include the following information:

Project Name: [insert name]

Funding Organization: [insert name of the grantor]

Funding Use: [insert a general statement]

Supporting Evidence: [insert facts supporting your rationale and need for the funding]

Supporting Research: [insert one or two research articles supporting the rationale]

Personal Story: Write a short narrative describing the problem and a solution from the point of view of a student / teacher / parent. [insert details for the story]

Funding Organization: [insert the name of the grantor]

Funding Organization Priorities: [insert the funding priorities of the grantor]

Budget Narrative Template

> Write a Persuasive budget narrative for the grant proposal.
>
> Project Name: [insert name]
>
> Direct Costs: funds required for the project, followed by the estimated amount.
>
> Program materials: $[insert cost]
>
> Staff stipends: $[insert cost]
>
> Indirect Costs: funds necessary to reach the best results, followed by estimated amounts.
>
> Program materials: $[insert cost]
>
> Staff stipends: $[insert cost]

Summary or Abstract

> Write a summary or an abstract of the grant using the information created in this stream of conversation.

⎯⎯⎯⎯• A CAUTION

Although using AI to write grants can be efficient and fast, it is important to review and edit the proposals generated by the software to ensure accuracy. AI can help write grant proposals by generating compelling drafts, but human input and expertise are crucial for success. Grant writers should always make sure the final proposal reflects their vision and experiences.

AI can give helpful information and make things more efficient, but it shouldn't replace working together, thinking creatively, and writing persuasively. These skills are important for a strong grant proposal. Only when AI and human grant writers work together can they create more effective grant proposals and gain a higher chance of securing the award.

14. Design Interview Questions for a New Hire

 THE PROBLEM

Interview Issues

Crafting good interview questions for a panel to ask a candidate is an important and time-consuming task. The questions must assess the skills, qualities, and qualifications needed for the job to prevent hiring the wrong people. Poorly crafted or generic questions can fail to reveal a candidate's true potential, which can lead to uninformed or misguided hiring decisions. Mismatches can create increased turnover and higher recruitment costs.

 THE SOLUTION

Compelling Queries

AI tools are excellent for generating accurate, objective, and engaging interview questions for an interview panel, helping to make better hiring choices and find the right people for the campus and role. To ensure the questions are effective, it is important to be clear in the prompt about the purpose of the interview. Also, use a variety of question types and tailor the questions to the specific role.

 AN EXAMPLE

This example is a prompt written to target a specific role.

> Our campus team of educators is interviewing candidates for the role of a school librarian / media specialist. Create four interview questions assessing the following traits: [insert traits, e.g., organized, culture fit, growth mindset, learning ability and adaptability]. Add an answer key for each question that provides suggested responses based on evidence-based research.

These examples align with ISTE Standard 3.3.c, Inspire a Culture of Innovation, which states, "Inspire a culture of innovation and collaboration that allows the time and space to explore and experiment with digital tools and adoption."

ACCELERATION

Adding a hands-on component to the interview is a great way to get to know candidates better. AI-powered platforms can generate a variety of simulations for the school setting that let candidates show off their skills and talents in a more practical and realistic way.

Create 1 technical assignment to use in an interview process for a candidate seeking the job of [insert role, e.g., librarian / media specialist]. The purpose of the exercise is to test their technical ability. Include a checklist of what to look for to complete the task successfully.

Consider incorporating situational questions. The AI tool will generate questions to assess critical skills in real-life scenarios. Find out how candidates would handle challenges relevant to the role.

Create 5 situational questions for the interview. Incorporate a scenario reflecting a common issue for a [insert role, e.g., librarian / media specialist]. Ask how the candidate in the interview would handle the challenge. Include a checklist of what to listen for in the answers.

Discussion Questions: Collaborative Decision-Making

Using AI in collaborative decision-making can help you achieve better and more equitable results. Consider using the reflective questions provided below. The conversations will foster greater cohesion as a team and enhance your collective decision-making skills.

1. How do you ensure everyone's opinion is respected and included when making decisions together? How can AI help with this?

2. When do you realize you need a checklist, and how does it help you at work or when you are making decisions?

3. Can you recall a vision or mission statement from any of your previous jobs? Based on your memory of the statement, what does it tell you about the importance and impact of the visioning process?

4. How many questions are needed to make a discussion group have interesting and meaningful conversations? What topics do we need to explore?

Chapter 4

SUPPORTIVE RELATIONSHIPS AND TRUST

THROUGHOUT MY CAREER, I've had the privilege of leading in several unique settings, ranging from individual campuses to the central office. Regardless of the specific context, one constant remained: the crucial role of trust in building healthy relationships. This process wasn't about quick fixes. It was about intentionally connecting with educators, fostering a sense of safety and mutual respect.

In one experience, I inherited a school struggling with low morale and a fractured sense of community. Teachers felt unsupported and students disengaged. My initial focus was building trust rather than curriculum or standardized tests. I started by scheduling one-on-one meetings with every educator—not for evaluations, but for open conversations. I actively listened to their concerns, frustrations, and ideas. Slowly, walls began to come down. Over time, a sense of camaraderie emerged. Teachers felt valued and heard, translating into a renewed commitment to their students.

Leaders who prioritize healthy relationships understand that a supportive environment built on trust is essential for educators to thrive. This, in turn, directly benefits student learning. While AI can be a powerful tool for automating tasks and organizing information, its true value lies in creating more space for those essential human connections. When implemented thoughtfully, AI can free up valuable time for leaders to engage in genuine conversations, fostering authentic communication with their staff. This, in turn, fosters an environment that aligns with the ISTE Education Leader Standards, specifically 3.1, Equity and Citizenship Advocate, and 3.3, Empowering Leader.

The following chapters will provide practical examples that demonstrate how to cultivate these qualities. You'll find strategies that embody ISTE Standard 3.1.c, which emphasizes a leader's role in modeling digital citizenship, and 3.1.d, which promotes responsible online behavior and ethical technology use. Additionally, the chapter explores practices that align with ISTE Standard 3.3.c, fostering a supportive and innovative culture through collaboration and constructive feedback, and 3.3.d, setting up learning opportunities that cater to the diverse needs of all.

Connection to the ISTE Standards for Leaders

3.1 Equity and Citizenship Advocate
Leaders use technology to increase equity, inclusion and digital citizenship practices.

3.1.c Model digital citizenship by critically evaluating online resources, engaging in civil discourse online and using digital tools to contribute to positive social change.

3.1.d Cultivate responsible online behavior, including the safe, ethical and legal use of technology.

3.3 Empowering Leader
Leaders create a culture where teachers and learners are empowered to use technology in innovative ways to enrich teaching and learning.

3.3.c Inspire a culture of innovation and collaboration that allows the time and space to explore and experiment with digital tools. and adoption.

3.3.d Support educators in using technology to advance learning that meets the diverse learning, cultural and social-emotional needs of individual students.

By prioritizing trust-based relationships, we can create a thriving school environment where both educators and students feel empowered to succeed.

15. Build a Culture of Celebration and Support

 THE PROBLEM

Shallow Slogans and Swag

Many teachers love "jeans day," but they aren't looking for just surface-level treats to feel appreciated. What they really want is to be respected and have their needs and ideas taken seriously. Recognition does not come just from slogans or swag; it comes from feeling you are a whole person—seen, heard, and truly understood. Neglecting to recognize and support your teachers during good times or bad can lead to feelings of isolation and neglect. You risk alienating valuable members of your community if it seems no one cares. This can lead to a decrease in overall well-being and productivity. Supporting strong relationships and a healthy campus culture is not just a luxury—it is a necessity.

 THE SOLUTION

A Culture of Care

Healthy schools have a wellness committee. They work together to suggest and plan events. They also coordinate logistics and evaluate success. While I was a principal, our campus team called themselves the "Culture and Care Team." We gathered suggestions reflecting the unique needs of our campus. The committee helped support health or family changes and came up with ideas for shared experiences and celebrations. Cultivating a culture of care means taking action. So, when you're looking for a way to strengthen community vibes, enlist an AI assistant to brainstorm ideas with a wellness team.

 AN EXAMPLE

Encourage your wellness committee to use an AI assistant to create a guidebook for their work. It will skyrocket their success. Try using this prompt as a template, adding details to align with your campus needs.

This example illustrates ISTE Standard 3.3.c, Inspire a Culture of Innovation, which states, "Inspire a culture of innovation and collaboration that allows the time and space to explore and experiment with digital tools and adoption."

> Write a guidebook for the Wellness Committee of our school using the following information:
>
> Purpose, Goals, and Name of Committee: [insert purpose and goals]
>
> Celebrations for Individuals: [insert events, e.g., retirement, birthday, marriage, birth, bosses' day, secretary's day]
>
> Celebrations as a Group: [insert events, e.g., staff appreciation, volunteer appreciation]
>
> Events Coordinated: [list events]
>
> Communication: [insert details, e.g., staff members will inform the committee about health issues and special news, contact a member of the committee with an email]
>
> Health Issues Supported: [insert details, e.g., hospitalization, sickness, death]
>
> Donations Collected (from the community and parent organization): [insert $ amount]
>
> Contributions Collected (from staff members for flowers, cards, or gifts): [insert $ amount]

 ACCELERATION

Create a Form to Collect Individual Preferences

Showing genuine care during the big or small wins in life amplifies wellness on campus. Gathering information about staff members can help customize acknowledgments and events. Use this prompt to create a digital survey to collect information. Or if you want the survey formatted to print on paper, include this phrase, "Format the survey to print on A4 paper."

> Create a form for a school-wide wellness team to collect individual preferences. Include the following prompts and questions to celebrate and support the campus staff during significant individual life events. Include a note of assurance explaining how information will be kept confidential and only be used by the committee to strengthen a healthy campus culture.
>
> First name; last name; grade level or department; home mailing address; personal cell phone number
>
> Birthday month and day
>
> Hospital of choice
>
> Possible events expected this year: a) birth/adoption, b) marriage, c) other
>
> Sweet treat favorite; drink favorite; flower favorite; gift card favorite
>
> Anything else you want the committee to know

Create a Shared Calendar

Celebrations are important. They can boost morale, build community, and relieve stress. But when a campus leader becomes a regular party pooper and does not take time to celebrate, things can go south. Stress becomes the icing on a not-so-fun cake. Morale deflates like a lifeless balloon. Not exactly the best environment for learning or working, right?

An AI assistant can help your wellness team come up with fun celebration ideas. It is a whiz at planning —think venue suggestions, decor ideas, and even interactive activities to keep things lively. Want a customized event calendar? Add your preferences into the prompt, and you will get a tailored monthly calendar highlighting milestones, holidays, and other big days. Make each occasion special by including the campus's unique traits and traditions in the plan. This will make the celebrations enjoyable and meaningful for everyone who works there.

> Create a year-long calendar of ways to celebrate with a school faculty from August through May. Include at least three ideas a month for unique celebrations on campus, such as [include details unique to your campus]. Include one optional off-campus event in the fall and one in the spring.

Create a Wellness Wishlist

Use this next prompt with your wellness team to jazz things up with a creative checklist. Experiment by presenting this prompt to various chatbots and contrasting their responses. Remember to engage in a dialogue with the AI chatbot by providing examples or requesting multiple ideas. Also, allow your faculty to rank their preferences or contribute their own ideas. Just be prepared for them to request a salary increase—which these days makes sense.

> Create a fun checklist for our school campus. It will list stress-free ways to bring some healthy energy into the campus. The goal is to check off all items on the "Wellness Wishlist" before the end of the school year. The list is designed to build rapport and focus on a healthy, joyful, and fun working environment. Number the list.

16. Cultivate Trust with Structured Feedback

 **THE PROBLEM**

Stressful Feedback Frenzy

When I reflect on my early days as a new teacher, observations were stressful. On one hand, I was excited to show off what my students had learned. But on the flip side, I was a bit on edge, worrying about what might go wrong or what might not be up to par. I remember my very first time teaching kindergarteners about letter sounds. If you've ever taught five-year-olds, you know it can be challenging—like herding a pack of hyperactive kittens. As soon as the principal came in, I lost my excitement and started feeling nervous. I stumbled over my words and doubted myself. That post-observation chat? I wasn't looking forward to it.

Receiving feedback, as Myung and Martinez (2013, p. 4) note, can trigger our fight-or-flight response, akin to facing a lion. This often leads to stress in teachers during pre- or post-observation discussions with a supervisor, which are meant to be constructive. Stress elevates our levels to the point where our brain shifts into a survival state that is not conducive to learning. When feedback seems erratic and unpredictable, it compounds the challenge of establishing a learning environment. Without a coherent feedback strategy from school leaders, teachers may become resistant to new ideas, feel uncertain, and respond with defensiveness or complete withdrawal.

 THE SOLUTION

Structured Sessions for Success

One way to alleviate stress in post-observation meetings is to use a structured protocol. A carefully planned approach can make post-observation meetings more predictable and ease teachers' jitters. With the help of AI, you can guide discussions teachers not only appreciate but also find practically useful in their work.

According to Justin Baeder (2017), meeting with a supervisor is not about passing or failing. It's also not just about getting a to-do list. Real growth is about reflection, introspection, and taking charge of our own learning. Instead of the boss doling out the "right answers," they should nudge us into deep thought and personal insights (Baeder, 2017).

How exactly can an AI thought partner help you with this process? The AI chatbot can help craft deep-dive questions for impactful feedback. It can help you sift through and spotlight the key insights to supercharge your discussions. And, after working through the structure with the chatbot, you'll have more time to dial back on the paperwork and focus on connecting as only humans know how to do.

 AN EXAMPLE

In this example, I fed AI my observation notes. The notes helped the AI create questions and topics about the teacher's lesson. I also included the content from a template designed by Baeder called "10 Questions for Better Teaching Feedback." You can find the questions as a free resource on The Principal Center's website (2017). In his 2017 book, *Now We're Talking,* Baeder emphasizes a move away from dispensing feedback to promoting self-reflection among teachers. In the example below, the prompt asks the AI assistant to create customized questions for a teacher conference using observation notes, objectives, and Baeder's structured template.

 You are a supervisor who has just observed a teacher. You took notes during the observation and are planning a one-on-one meeting with an educator to provide time for reflection and feedback. Use the 10-point structure to customize a list of 10 questions. Incorporate the notes from the observation into the questions. Insert details from the observation notes inside the brackets [ ].

NOTES FROM THE OBSERVATION: [insert observation notes typed during the observation].

STRUCTURE FOR QUESTIONS:

Context: I noticed your lesson objective is [ ]. Could you talk to me about how the objective aligns with your lesson?

Perception: Here's what I saw the students doing [ ]. Tell me about what you thought about those actions.

Interpretation: At one point in the lesson, it seemed that [ ]. What was your take on this moment?

Decision: Tell me about this point in the lesson when you decided to [ ]. What went into your decision?

Comparison: I noticed students were [ ]. How did this compare with what you expected to happen when you planned the lesson?

Antecedent: I noticed that [ ] happened. Could you tell me about what led up to this moment, perhaps in a previous lesson?

Adjustment: I saw [ ]. What did you think of this moment? Will it affect what you do tomorrow?

Intuition: I noticed [ ]. How did you feel about how this portion of the lesson played out?

Alignment: I noticed [ ]. What connections do you see to your objective for the lesson?

Impact: What effect did you think it had when [ ] happened?

This example illustrates ISTE Standard 3.3.c, Inspire a Culture of Innovation, which states, "Inspire a culture of innovation and collaboration that allows the time and space to explore and experiment with digital tools and adoption."

 •——— **ACCELERATION**

Using Another Structure

For this example, I gave the AI my notes and asked it to use the content in Paul Bambrick-Santoyo's six-step feedback guide in his book, *Leverage Leadership* (2017). Combine your observation notes with this content, and you will receive conversation questions tailored to the situation. The questions will help keep the conversation going and promote interaction for a supportive session.

> Provide a set of questions for a feedback session with a teacher and their supervisor who has observed the lesson. Use the structured template provided. The questions must incorporate the observation notes provided. Also, offer one suggestion for each step in the structure provided. Use a tone of inquiry aligned with a sense of collaboration rather than authoritative advice.
>
> Structure for Questioning and Feedback:
>
> Praise something done well
>
> Probe for an area of improvement
>
> Identify problem and action steps
>
> Practice with role-play
>
> Design a plan
>
> Set timeline for follow-up
>
> Notes from the observation: [insert your notes].

Conducting Pre-Conference Discussions

In *Now We're Talking*, Baeder illustrates a common error made during observation. Often the observer does not focus on whether the lesson accomplishes what the teacher intended. "This leads to frustration and resistance from teachers who may be genuinely interested in feedback. If we enter each classroom with an open mind, we can focus on addressing the issues that are most relevant to the teacher" (Baeder 2017, pg. 19). This is one of the reasons why pre-conference conversations are important. Let an AI craft suggestions for a pre-conference, and it can help the process of evaluations validate the teacher's intent.

Write a set of questions for a pre-conference discussion with a teacher held prior to any formal observations. Focus the questions on self-reflection, goal setting, and stress relief. Give the principal suggestions on how to use active listening techniques.

Summarizing Information for Follow-Up

Your AI assistant can also help by suggesting language for an email to follow up on the feedback session.

 Create a summarizing email to a teacher from the supervisor who has just conducted a post-conference meeting about an observation on [insert date]. Summarize the notes: [insert notes].

Use this outline:

Something done well

An identified action step

A designated plan of action

A set timeline for follow-up

Write with a tone of gratitude and encouragement.

Schedule an additional appointment for [insert date].

 A CAUTION

The AI assistant can generate many, many suggestions. But this does not mean you need to use them all. Bombarding teachers with too much information or too many questions can backfire. Pre- and post-conference sessions aim to promote growth. But if you offer a laundry list of advice, the teacher might feel as if she is drinking from a fire hose. Those who receive too many suggestions for improvement may walk away discouraged instead of motivated to change. Try focusing on one specific goal generated by the teacher rather than trying to "fix" everything at once.

17. Resolve Issues with Restorative Circles

 THE PROBLEM

Tension and Distrust

Schools are similar to small towns; there will be conflict and disagreements. Conflicts can happen between teachers, students, or parents and school staff. When people interact, misunderstandings will inevitably pop up. Disagreements can affect the climate in a school and can manifest in a variety of ways. Trust starts to drop, teachers get downhearted, and sometimes big issues don't get the attention they need. This kind of tension can create splits in the school family. It's not just about hurt feelings, either. If things get really bad, the school's reputation could take a hit, and problems might spiral out of hand.

 THE SOLUTION

Healing Circles

To bridge these divides, you may want to turn to a strategy called Restorative or Healing Circles. AI technology can be a valuable ally when using this structure.

If you want to learn about Restorative Circles, ask your AI tutor. They can explain and give you resources to study and get support. Or prompt it to generate suggestions that ensure the process is safe and inclusive.

The AI assistant can suggest questions to jump-start important and healing conversations. These critical discussions are crucial in solving problems and creating a peaceful school. With the help of the AI assistant, Restorative Circles can foster health and unity in schools.

 AN EXAMPLE

Use the AI as a personal tutor to learn more about the strategy.

> I'm interested in implementing Restorative Circles to improve the culture and conflict resolution on our school campus. Provide an overview of Restorative Circles, including their principles and how they differ from traditional approaches. I'm particularly interested in how Restorative Circles can be applied to address [insert the specific issue, e.g., adult or student conflicts]. Additionally, recommend practical resources, such as guides, best practices, case studies from schools that have successfully implemented them, and training programs available for educators.

After you understand how it works, you can ask the AI to create questions for a particular situation. In this example, the prompt generates questions to guide a discussion on bullying. When you craft the prompt, think about the participants' grade level or age group. Include information about how the group interacts. Note that this prompt uses a structure to guide the content of the questions. Most importantly, evaluate the questions provided by AI and choose those that will help contribute to positive social change.

Create a list of questions for a Restorative Circle focused on addressing bully behaviors on the playground. The purpose of this Restorative Circle is to foster understanding, growth, and positive change within the student community. These questions should be appropriate for fifth grade students. Your goal is to promote open dialogue, empathy, and understanding among the students. Ensure your questions are age-appropriate and easy to understand, using language that fosters inclusivity, respect, and empathy. Use the following structure as you create your list:

1. ICEBREAKER: Start with an icebreaker question to help students feel comfortable and engaged. Then include an opening script for the leader, which sets the stage for the Restorative Circle dialogue.

2. REFLECTION: Include questions to encourage reflection on personal experiences with bullying, both as targets and witnesses.

3. IMPACT: Ask about the impact of bullying, exploring emotions felt by those involved and the broader school community.

4. PREVENTION: Discuss strategies for preventing and responding to bullying situations.

5. SUPPORT: Encourage students to consider ways to support each other and promote a positive and inclusive playground environment.

6. BYSTANDERS: Create opportunities for students to share their thoughts on the role of bystanders in bullying situations.

This example illustrates ISTE Standard 3.1.c, Model Digital Citizenship, which states, "Model digital citizenship by critically evaluating online resources, engaging in civil discourse online and using digital tools to contribute to positive social change."

ACCELERATION

Restorative Circles can help adults resolve conflicts constructively and respectfully. By providing a safe space to share, Restorative Circles can help to clear up confusion and build trust. Restorative Circles promote open communication and collaboration, strengthening relationships and achieving shared goals. Try using this prompt with your AI assistant for a specific situation.

> Write a list of questions to use in the Restorative Circle to help resolve a conflict between two adults who have an issue: [insert details, e.g., having difficulty working together].
>
> The goal of the Restorative Circle session is to help resolve a conflict effectively. The purpose of this Restorative Circle is to foster understanding, growth, and change. The outcome should help the participants understand each other's perspectives and find a solution that works for both. Provide a description of the activity, ground rules, and any tips for facilitating a Restorative Circle with adults.

18. Document a Delicate Issue

THE PROBLEM

Documentation Dilemma

Ensuring a safe and positive school environment requires addressing inappropriate adult behavior, whether it violates school rules or even the law. However, navigating this process can be a significant challenge for school leaders. Difficult conversations with staff members are emotionally draining and time-consuming, further compounded by the burden of thorough documentation. Manual report writing takes an excessive amount of time, often leading to delays that can jeopardize the school's legal position should a dispute arise. Furthermore, incomplete or inaccurate records can damage the school's reputation and erode trust with staff, students, and the community.

Beyond the logistical hurdles, a purely punitive approach to staff misconduct can be unfruitful. When the focus is solely on documenting mistakes, valuable opportunities for improvement are missed. Employees caught breaking rules or engaging in inappropriate behavior deserve a chance to reflect on their actions and develop strategies for better decision-making in the future.

THE SOLUTION

Streamlined Strategy

Administrators can leverage technology to create a clear and consistent approach to documenting adult interactions. AI-powered templates offer customizable sections to capture the meeting's purpose, any allegations or concerns, supporting evidence, employee responses, and potential disciplinary actions. This streamlines the process, promotes factual and unbiased documentation, and ensures everyone is held accountable.

Reflective practice should be integrated throughout the documentation process. After using the templates, administrators can take time to reflect on: 1) The tone and objectivity of the documentation, 2) whether all relevant information is captured, and 3) if the documentation promotes a fair and transparent process. By reflecting on these questions, administrators can ensure they are using technology effectively to create accurate and professional documentation that upholds trust and strengthens relationships with staff members. It's important to remember that these templates are just a starting point. Feel free to customize them to fit your school's policies and legal requirements. The goal is to make the process as smooth as possible for everyone involved.

 AN EXAMPLE

These templates provide suggestions for documenting adult conflicts and issues in a school setting. Remember to tailor the documents to fit your specific circumstances. These examples align with ISTE Standard 3.5.c, Engage in Reflective Practice, which states, "Use technology to regularly engage in reflective practices that support personal and professional growth."

Investigative Template

Before taking any corrective measures, hold a conversation with all those involved. The administrator can hear everyone's perspective, evaluate the seriousness, and then document a fair plan using a specific template.

 Create a form / template to be printed on A4 paper. The form will be used to document a meeting with employees who were involved in a conflict on campus. The meeting is designed as an investigation of this issue [insert the issue, e.g., allegations of harassment, bullying, or theft].

The purpose of the meeting is to gather information, take statements, and ensure a fair process. This meeting is held before making disciplinary decisions. Include ways to maintain healthy relationships while also addressing the matter seriously.

The form should encourage open dialogue, provide space for individual accounts, and ensure all parties feel heard and respected throughout the investigation process. Include a section for signatures of all involved in the meeting.

Written Warning Template

Once the facts are gathered and it is time to take action regarding the employee(s), this prompt can assist by giving suggestions for recording the meeting.

Create a form to be printed on A4 paper. This document is a template used in a meeting with a school employee who [insert the issue, e.g., habitual tardiness or unacceptable work performance]. A prior conversation has occurred, but the issue has persisted.

The purpose of the meeting is a formal warning. These key items are needed in the form:

The employee's name, job title, and date of the incident.

A brief description of the incident.

The evidence that supports the allegations against the employee.

The specific corrective action to follow.

The reason for the corrective action.

The employee's response to the allegations and the disciplinary action.

The signatures of all involved in the meeting.

Suggest content for each item in the form. Include ways to maintain the relationship while also addressing the matter seriously.

The form should encourage open dialogue, provide space for individual accounts, and ensure all parties feel heard and respected throughout the process.

Performance Improvement Plan (PIP) Template

Create a form to be printed on A4 paper. This document is a template used to record a meeting with a school employee who [insert issue such as habitual tardiness or unacceptable work performance]. The template will serve as a Performance Improvement Plan. This plan outlines specific areas where the employee needs to improve, provides a timeline for review, and details potential consequences if the desired improvement is not met. Suggest content for each item in the form. The form should encourage open dialogue, provide space for individual accounts, and ensure all parties feel heard and respected. Include a section for signatures of all involved in the meeting.

Suspension Template

Create a form to be printed on A4 paper. This document is a template used to document a meeting with a school employee who has [insert issue]. The employee will be suspended [either with or without pay]. The suspension meeting will detail the reasons for the suspension, its duration, and the expectations upon return. Suggest content for each item in the form. The form should encourage open dialogue, provide space for individual accounts, and ensure all parties feel heard and respected. Include a section for signatures of all involved in the meeting.

Appeal Template

Create a form to be printed on A4 paper. This document is a template used to record a meeting with a school employee who wants to appeal disciplinary actions taken against them. An appeal meeting lets the employee present their case and any evidence to reconsider the decision. Suggest content for each item in the form. The form should encourage open dialogue, provide space for individual accounts, and ensure all parties feel heard and respected. Include a section for signatures of all involved in the meeting.

Termination Template

Create a form to be printed on A4 paper. This document is a template used to document a termination meeting for a school employee. This meeting is occurring after all other disciplinary measures fail or in the case of gross misconduct. The document provides a formal written notification of termination. This meeting communicates the decision to the employee, the reasons for the termination, and any logistical details such as final pay, benefits, etc. Suggest content for each item in the form. Include a section for signatures of all involved in the meeting.

 A CAUTION

Please note: any template generated by an AI assistant should be adapted as necessary to fit the specific legal and institutional requirements of your campus, district, or organization. It is a best practice to seek advice from HR professionals or legal experts when finalizing a template so that it aligns with your school's disciplinary procedures. Review and tailor each template according to your organization's policies, practices, and culture. Avoid providing personal or identifying information in the prompt for the AI assistant.

19. Support Student Behavior

 THE PROBLEM

Conduct Conundrum

As someone who has been both a teacher and a school leader, I understand the complex challenges of student behavior in schools. Behavior issues can be demanding even for experienced educators. Students' emotional needs can sometimes overwhelm the primary focus of teaching and learning. Maintaining a healthy school environment is about more than just rule enforcement. It involves managing a range of personalities, backgrounds, and unexpected issues.

 THE SOLUTION

Smart Support for Students

By combining the power of AI with a strategic plan that addresses the root causes of behavior issues, fosters social-emotional learning, and prioritizes human expertise, schools can create a more positive and productive learning environment for all students. AI tools can identify trends, create personalized plans, measure the effectiveness of different methods, and more.

These examples align with ISTE Standard 3.3.d, Use Tech to Meet Student Learning Needs, which states, "Support educators in using technology to advance learning that meets the diverse learning, cultural and social-emotional needs of individual students."

 AN EXAMPLE

If not addressed, bullying on the playground can disrupt a student's sense of safety and enjoyment at school. In the following prompt, AI will provide tailored approaches to address this issue, along with other support.

> Suggest five tailored approaches to address a trend of bullying incidents occurring on the elementary school playground. [Insert general descriptions, e.g., pushing, shaming, ostracizing others]. Provide suggestions for programs to use with teachers, strategies for students, and ways to involve parents in creating more positive and inclusive interactions during recess or unstructured play.

 **ACCELERATION**

Here are a few more ideas to try with your handy AI assistant.

Identify Patterns

AI can find patterns of misbehavior in student discipline records. The records must be de-identified before being entered into the prompt. Certain misbehaviors may happen more frequently at certain times of the day or in specific places. Or there might be students who are frequently disruptive and removed from class. AI will observe these patterns and advise how to improve the student's behavior and strategies for school. The analysis helps target interventions and consequences more effectively.

 Examine this report and detect any overarching trends or patterns. Specifically, look for patterns associated with individual students, such as whether a student's disruptive behavior intensifies around particular times of the day or locations. [Insert a de-identified spreadsheet].

Identify Stress and Mental Health Indicator

As educators, it's important to identify the underlying reasons behind disruptive student behaviors, such as talking out of turn, not following directions, or physical aggression. The following prompt examines specific actions captured from referrals for individualized support sessions. The goal is to identify signs of stress, concerns, or outside challenges that might be impacting the student. Additionally, it aims to identify ways to support students and prevent disruptions in the classroom.

 Review the following description of student behavior. Suggest data that can help to pinpoint possible indicators of stress, concerns, or external factors impacting the student. Propose evidence-based practices based to inform this issue. The goal is to identify signs of stress, concerns, or outside challenges that might be impacting the student and ways to support students to prevent classroom disruptions. [Deidentify details from reports provided by the adult(s) working with the student].

Build Student Awareness About Behavior

Students with chronic discipline issues sometimes lack the skills and knowledge to comprehend why they do what they do. By understanding how their body works during challenging or stressful situations, they may develop skills to change their behavior for the better.

Using the CASEL definitions, explain self-awareness and self-regulation to a 10-year-old fourth grade student. Write a script explaining how the student can use this information. Explain how they can learn to change their behavior in the moment. Teach them how the amygdala in the brain is reactionary but can be regulated. Provide a visual of the brain's amygdala, if available.

Suggest Targeted Professional Learning Programs

AI can provide suggestions for campus teams who are responsible for managing student behavior by offering a variety of researched-based practices. AI can serve as a guide through the process, suggesting actions and offering resources or materials. If you are searching for an evidence-based practice, try this prompt.

 List evidence-based practices that support behavior management and discipline in schools that can be used with a school faculty during a professional learning session. Provide a summary and resources available online.

Facilitate the Learning Process for a Teacher or Team

Here are two more prompts illustrating how AI can facilitate a learning session about a specific topic. The suggestions will help the team by giving them a place to share ideas and seek advice.

 Using the evidence-based practice of [insert title, e.g. Positive Behavior Interventions and Supports (PBIS)], provide 6 open-ended questions tailored for a student to prompt reflection on their behavior. Craft the questions to match the student's reading level. Include suggested consequences for the student. Consider the following details about the student:

Age: [Provide Age]

Grade: [Provide Grade]

Reading level: [Provide Reading Level]

Known social or emotional issue: [Specify issue, e.g., bully behavior in the cafeteria]

 Functional behavior assessment is a process used to identify the function of a student's misbehavior. This information can develop interventions to address the underlying need driving the misbehavior. Using FBA, provide guidance for a campus team on how to navigate these practices effectively. Suggest relevant actions and recommend resources or materials for implementing the assessment.

Create Communication Templates

AI can personalize communication with students and parents. Use it to write letters or emails to parents, guardians, or stakeholders about disciplinary incidents. Make sure the communication is clear, consistent, and follows school policies. This approach helps everyone feel more aligned and supported.

> Craft a template for an email directed to a parent or guardian regarding a disciplinary incident at school. Ensure the content is clear and consistent, aiming to foster understanding and support for both students and parents. The goal is to maintain transparent communication, ensuring everyone involved is well-informed and feels valued.

This prompt will create a template to record discipline referrals in a Student Behavior Report. Try using this prompt with Google's Gemini to export directly to the spreadsheet. Teachers can then use the form when they complete a student referral report. The form would be shared only with school administration to document information.

> Create a template for a spreadsheet that teachers can use to communicate behavior issues that need administrator support. Include the following information as column headers for the spreadsheet: Last name of student, First name, Date of issue, Time of issue, Location, Description, Any witnesses, Actions taken with the teacher, Notes. Provide one row with an example.

TEMPLATE: Sunshine Elem Behavior Report

File Edit View Insert Format Data Tools Extensions Help

B2 — fx Smith

	Last name	First name	Date of issue	Time of issue	Location	Description	Any witnesses	Actions taken with the teacher	Notes
EXAMPLE	Smith	John	2023-08-20	10:00 AM	Classroom	Threw a book at another student	Jane Doe, John Doe	Sent the student to the principal's office	Will follow up with the student and their parents to discuss why they threw the book and how we can prevent this from happening again.

FIGURE 4.1 This Behavior Report Form is a Google Sheet created by Gemini. It illustrates a template with headers and an example entry.

Analyze Feedback

The next prompt will help you analyze feedback from students, parents, and teachers. Gathered through surveys and focus groups, the feedback is anonymous. This prompt aims to understand the effectiveness of current practices.

Analyze this feedback from students, parents, and teachers about disciplinary actions [insert anonymous feedback from surveys or focus groups].

Track the Effectiveness of Interventions and Consequences

You can use this prompt to see how certain actions affect student behavior. The aim is to study and find connections between the behaviors and the use of specific actions. This might apply to peer mentoring sessions or specific programs. To better understand students' behavior, it can be helpful to note if these behaviors increase during exams or when they are stressed. Only use non-identifiable student behavior data to maintain privacy and confidentiality.

Given the following dataset detailing student behavioral incidents over a school year, analyze and identify any patterns or correlations between implementing [insert intervention, e.g., peer mentoring sessions] and reducing [insert behavior, e.g., classroom disruptions].

[Insert non-identifiable student behavior data].

Then note if this behavior increases during certain times of the year, such as exam periods [insert dates of exams].

Policy Recommendations

This prompt can assist in evaluating and enhancing existing school discipline policies. The AI assistant will review the current policies and find areas that need improvement. It can also suggest revisions that are fair and effective. Notice the prompt asks for positive presupposition. The emphasis is on moving away from punitive language and toward a more constructive and supportive approach.

Review the current school discipline policies, suggesting possible revisions. Highlight areas for improvement. Write descriptions that are comprehensive, fair, and effective. The text should reflect positive presuppositions. [insert discipline policy or other documents explaining the policy].

A CAUTION

When writing a prompt, you must remove all personal identifying information. To protect privacy, replace student names with a unique identifier before asking the AI to analyze discipline reports. This can be a random number or a letter combination. It is also important to remember AI is not a substitute for the human touch and personal judgment of school leaders. AI is a valuable tool, but it cannot replace empathy and understanding. When considering recommendations, take into account each student's unique circumstances and needs.

20. Write with Purpose and Tone

THE PROBLEM

Robo-Response Regrets

Some people worry about sounding fake or cold when using a machine for personal messages. Automated emails are quick and easy, but they can come off as insincere or robotic, leading to misinterpretations of the message or a lack of connection with the person.

THE SOLUTION

Your Digital Scribe

To ensure the AI assistant sounds like you, give it instructions and a writing sample. Provide an example of your writing style. Over time, it will gain the capacity to adjust. This also means the response you get today may look different from what you receive in the future. This ability to adopt a personalized approach is a powerful AI strategy. Experiment with various tones and styles of writing. Try using some of these terms in the prompt, such as professional, persuasive, formal, informal, casual, descriptive, humorous, friendly, academic, firm, confident, or poetic.

AN EXAMPLE

Ask the AI assistant to analyze samples of your writing to understand your style and tone. Then test it out in response to an email.

These examples align with ISTE Standard 3.5.d, Navigate Continuous Improvement, which states, "Develop the skills needed to lead and navigate change, advance systems and promote a mindset of continuous improvement for how technology can improve learning."

> Study this sample of how I write. SAMPLE EMAIL: [insert a sample of an email].
>
> Then write a response to this email from a teacher. TEACHER'S EMAIL [insert email].
>
> Generate a response in the same style and tone as my writing sample. Include the following tone: [insert terms matching your purpose, e.g., formal, empathetic, urgent].

 ACCELERATION

Several channels of communication are available to share information from a school. These include email, newsletters, blogs and recorded phone messages. Try enlisting an AI to help with one of your next messages.

A Message from the Principal

> You are the principal of a school. Draft a welcome letter and phone script for new students and their families. Introduce the leadership team and the school using these placeholders: Principal [name], Assistant Principal [name], [list other titles].
>
> Share the school's mission and values. [insert details].

A Message from the Teacher

You can offer the following prompts as examples to help your staff learn how to use an AI assistant in communication:

> You are a teacher of students in second grade. Write a template to use with mail merge for a monthly email to parents. This email will also be used to share important information about upcoming events or assignments. Write with a tone of gratitude for their support and your partnership to help their child succeed.

A Message from the Counselor

> You are a school counselor at the middle school campus. Write a letter to a student who is struggling. This letter needs to offer support and encouragement and help the student feel heard and understood

A Message for the Weekly Staff Newsletter or Blog

A weekly newsletter keeps everyone (who reads it) in the know. I offered a regularly updated digital newsletter called the "Echo Memo" that included new announcements and quick-access links to commonly referenced information.

I also wrote a weekly blog post on "The Echo Blog" to keep families informed. Readers enjoyed the updates, but writing the family newsletter and faculty blog took a long time. If only I'd had the help of an AI assistant back then to streamline the process. I would have tried a prompt such as the following.

> Write a series of messages for a newsletter to [insert audience, e.g., school staff, parents] with the following information:
> 1. Create a list of the upcoming events formatted in bullets [insert events, e.g., open house].
> 2. Create a list of the "bright spots" about good news on campus [insert details, e.g., Fishbowl strategy for thinking in writing was seen in Ms. Lawson's second grade class].
> 3. Write a 5-sentence paragraph on the topic of [insert topic, e.g., well-being].
> 4. Give me 5 quotes about the topic of [insert topic, e.g., collaboration].
> 5. Write a joke about school.

A Funny Line

If you're struggling to find a funny line to include in a message, you can ask the AI assistant to act as a comedian. If you want to be sarcastic with a close friend, you can use this example to get a response. I will admit it is a little over the top, but you get the gist. And if you don't want to use its first attempt, just tell the AI assistant to try again.

> Act like a comedian and respond sarcastically to a friend about how much I love to fill out reports.

 A CAUTION

Generative AI can sound like a chatty friend. It tries to sound natural and answer your questions in a way that will satisfy your request. But sometimes it makes mistakes and really misses the mark. The program learns from (and apologizes for) its errors. So always, always read over anything it writes to be sure it is saying what you want to say and how you want it to sound.

21. Recommend and Show Gratitude

 THE PROBLEM

Penning Praises on Paper

Writing letters of recommendation or thank you notes is an important yet often challenging task. Writing a meaningful message takes time. You need to collect information and think about the recipient's achievements. Finding the right words to show gratitude or support can be difficult. This is especially true when you're busy, and you might end up delaying or rushing your letters. If a letter does not seem real, it might not convey your message and could harm your relationship with the person you want to thank.

 THE SOLUTION

Wielding Words with Heart

David Steindl-Rast, a monk and interfaith scholar, suggests gratitude is the secret to a happy life (Steindl-Rast, 2013). So, let an AI assistant help expand your capacity for happiness by offering many more ways to express gratitude. If you need help writing a recommendation letter or a thank you email, this tool can assist you. An AI assistant is equipped to revise your drafted messages, ensuring your letters are polished and impactful. It can offer suggestions and enhance clarity, all while saving you time and effort.

 AN EXAMPLE

Express your appreciation, admiration, and support in a meaningful and cost-effective way. Let the words flow from the heart with a little help from the AI-powered digital wizard.

> Write a heartfelt thank you message to give to a teacher who provided muffins for the faculty meeting.

> Write a sample letter of recommendation for a second grade teacher. She has worked at Sunshine Elementary School for five years. [insert other details from her resume].

These examples align with ISTE Standard 3.5.d, Navigate Continuous Improvement, which states, "Develop the skills needed to lead and navigate change, advance systems and promote a mindset of continuous improvement for how technology can improve learning."

ACCELERATION

Include a Quote

Handwritten notes are a thoughtful and personal way to express gratitude or appreciation. Enhance your message by using an AI assistant to add more ideas, famous quotes, examples, metaphors, synonyms, or creative language. The AI assistant helps with new ideas and can remind you of important details you might have forgotten.

 Find 10 quotes about gratitude to include in a personal thank you note.

Send a Check-In Email or Text

A short email or a text can convey concern swiftly in the moment. If circumstances allow, a visit or phone call adds a more personal touch. Sending a quick email can help ease work-related concerns before reaching out more directly. When you use your AI thought partner regularly, it becomes a valuable asset for your writing. Try out these prompts to get an idea of the many ways an AI assistant can help you communicate with others.

 Write an email message to a teacher in the school faculty who is seriously ill. The teacher will miss a few weeks of work, so express empathy. Reassure that the students will be cared for in the teacher's absence and not to worry. Add that I will follow up with a phone call later in the week.

 Write a text to a colleague who is having a rough day. Find an image of a kitten to include with the message.

 Write an email highlighting a teacher's accomplishments and express gratitude for their hard work. Include a famous quote emphasizing the power of continual learning. [insert description of the teacher's accomplishment].

Discussion Questions:
Supportive Relationships and Trust

AI opens doors to new approaches for fostering supportive relationships and trust. The process can help create a healthier culture in your school community. Consider using the reflective questions below as a starting point for discussion. The conversations will help you and your team improve how you build the essential elements of relationships and trust.

1. Can you share an example of a well-crafted conversation that led to a positive outcome? What made it successful? How could AI assist in this situation?

2. How can feedback help build trust, collaboration, and accountability in a culture? How could AI have a role in crafting feedback?

3. When writing a brief and powerful summary, what elements make the summary meaningful and worth reading?

4. Can you recall a situation where the purpose and tone of an email had a significant impact? What lessons did you learn from it? How can AI help with this process?

5. When choosing questions for Restorative Circles, what types of questions do you include to promote dialogue and reflection?

6. How do you ensure your letters of recommendation and thank you notes are genuine and meaningful? What could an AI assistant help accomplish in this task?

Chapter 5

PERSONALIZED PROFESSIONAL LEARNING

AS AN EDUCATOR, LEARNING HAS ALWAYS been my guiding light. It's what initially drew me to the profession, and I knew it would be a career of continuous growth. How true that turned out to be! But the world of learning I entered decades ago, filled with textbooks and well-worn World Books, has been dramatically transformed by the arrival of the Internet and AI.

In the early years of school leadership, professional development often involved persuading educators, some more comfortable with traditional paper-and-pencil methods, to embrace new technologies. But with the advent of AI, the landscape shifted completely. Suddenly, learning has become a far more dynamic and personalized experience.

AI isn't a silver bullet, but the research is clear: when implemented effectively, it can produce incredible results. Studies have shown AI achieving scores of 90% on US bar exams and near-perfect scores on high school SAT math tests (Helmore, 2023). By embracing AI as a learning partner, we can unlock a world of possibilities, ensuring that educators like myself and future generations of educators are constantly equipped with the skills needed to guide students toward success.

AI is opening a world of new possibilities in education. This innovative technology has the potential to profoundly influence the way we learn and develop new skills.

ISTE Standard 3.5, Connected Learner, underscores chapter 5's focus on professional learning. The examples in this chapter align with an effort to foster a culture of continuous learning, leveraging advanced strategies to enhance teaching and learning. The topics advocate for a proactive approach to professional growth, emphasizing the role of technology in supporting educators' ability to lead, adapt, innovate, and thrive in a constantly evolving educational landscape.

Connection to the ISTE Standards for Leaders

3.5 Connected Learner
Leaders model and promote continuous professional learning for themselves and others.

- 3.5.a Set goals to remain current on emerging technologies for learning, innovations in pedagogy and advancements in the learning sciences.

- 3.5.b Participate regularly in online professional learning networks to collaboratively learn with and mentor other professionals.

- 3.5.c Use technology to regularly engage in reflective practices that support personal and professional growth.

- 3.5.d Develop the skills needed to lead and navigate change, advance systems and promote a mindset of continuous improvement for how technology can improve learning.

22. Write Goals the SMARTIE Way

THE PROBLEM

Goal Gridlock
Setting a clear direction and tracking progress is crucial for growth—but crafting goals can be daunting. Writing them is a meticulous task that can lead to feelings of frustration. If the goals are unmet, the process can be a major drain of time and energy. This gridlock can leave you discouraged and ready to throw in the towel.

THE SOLUTION

Goal Guidance

Stay in the ring and let AI coach you on how to write a few goals in a matter of minutes. AI can help you streamline the process so you have more time to focus on actually accomplishing the goals. It is especially good at crafting SMARTIE goals, which are Specific, Measurable, Achievable, Relevant, Time-bound, Inclusive, and Equitable.

When creating a prompt for a SMARTIE goal, stick to one specific objective, establish a timeline or deadline, and include how you want to measure your progress or success. To refine it, provide additional information in the same stream.

AN EXAMPLE

This prompt can help you write a goal suitable for a campus strategic plan. Start with the first prompt, then continue the conversation with the two additional prompts.

> Write a SMARTIE goal for [insert what you want to accomplish, e.g., building a healthy culture on my school campus through professional learning opportunities]. Make it Specific, Measurable, Achievable, Relevant, Time-bound, Inclusive and Equitable. My timeline is to accomplish this by [insert date] end of year, with a participation rate of [insert percentage] 98% of staff participating.

> Next, write one sentence combining all the elements.

> Now give three examples of professional learning sessions. These will serve as strategies for reaching this goal.

This example illustrates ISTE Standard 3.5.a, Stay Current on Innovation in Learning, which states, "Set goals to remain current on emerging technologies for learning, innovations in pedagogy and advancements in the learning sciences."

ACCELERATION

Goals for Prioritizing Growth and Connection

As a school leader, I had a specific goal to create time for my teachers to meet with me in regular one-on-one sessions. Initially, I dedicated the time to learning more about them. I encouraged them to do more of the talking while I listened. I found new teachers tended to focus on daily challenges such as time or classroom management. Those who were working parents sometimes discussed the difficulties of juggling responsibilities between work and home. My intent was to establish a culture of care by trying to understand each person as an individual. Eventually, the consistent and open communication built a sturdy bridge of trust for ideas to emerge. These sessions led to better and better results.

To write a specific goal for this initiative, try using an AI prompt such as this:

 Create a SMARTIE goal that helps me build a bridge of trust with my teachers. I want to improve communication and trust through one-on-one sessions. Make it Specific, Measurable, Achievable, Relevant, Time-bound, Inclusive and Equitable. Combine all the elements into one sentence.

Goals to Overcome Obstacles

Try this prompt when you need tailored strategies to help you overcome obstacles hindering you from reaching your goal.

 Suggest strategies to overcome barriers to my goal: [Insert goal].

23. Personalize Your Own PD

 **THE PROBLEM**

Pressed for Time

Recently, I was leading a workshop, and one participant introduced himself as a "Recovering Campus Principal"—a telling sign of our times. Researchers warn of a coming burnout crisis, not just for teachers but administrators too (DeMatthews, 2021). Many leaders I speak with express a deep commitment to supporting students and staff. However, despite their dedication and the impressive results they achieve under immense pressure, school leaders face an urgent need for solutions. The pandemic intensified already demanding workloads, leaving leaders constantly bombarded by unexpected issues. This relentless pressure creates a time crunch and makes it nearly impossible to tackle the critical issues that truly impact student learning. Solutions and resources exist, but where's the time to find them? How can school leaders delve deeper into solutions when they're drowning in information and struggling to stay afloat?

 THE SOLUTION

Recruit an AI Tutor

Imagine having an intelligent tutor astute enough to tailor lessons to your specific learning needs and provide personalized guidance and support throughout your educational journey. AI tools can swiftly sift through mountains of information, pinpointing relevant information and personalizing learning.

 AN EXAMPLE

In his book *The 80/20 Principle: The Secret to Achieving More with Less* (1999), Richard Koch argues most people waste their time and energy trying to learn everything about a subject, when in reality, they only need to learn the most important 20%. He says by focusing on the most important 20%, people can learn faster and achieve better results.

In the example below, the school leader seeks solutions to a specific topic. Enlist AI to explain the most important 20% of the topic. Apply the template in this prompt to any topic on your to-do list of things to learn.

> I want to learn more about [insert topic, e.g., collaborative leadership]. Identify the most important 20% of what I need to learn about the topic.

This example aligns with ISTE Standard 3.5.d, Navigate Continuous Improvement, which states, "Develop the skills needed to lead and navigate change, advance systems and promote a mindset of continuous improvement for how technology can improve learning."

 ACCELERATION

With AI's advanced search capabilities, you won't need to spend countless hours scrolling through the internet. Instead, you can receive tailored suggestions and summaries that provide the insights you need in a fraction of the time.

Design a Learning Journey

When you're ready to tackle a goal, let the AI chatbot serve as a personal learning coach, tutor, and thought partner. You will get an interesting interaction if you tell it to ask questions one at a time.

> I am a school leader and my goal is to learn more about [insert topic, e.g., managing Tier 3 student discipline]. Write a SMARTIE goal for me. Then act as a tutor to help me meet this goal. Ask me questions—one at a time—about the topic to determine what I need to know.

Compare Advantages and Disadvantages

> What are the advantages and disadvantages of [insert topic, e.g., restorative discipline]? Include recommended reading.

Locate Resources

> Help me find resources to read about this strategy [insert topic, e.g., using AI for communication]. Summarize how the strategy can work for a busy school leader. Include recommended reading.

Identify Trends

> Describe current trends and best practices for leading a school leadership team through a strategic plan for school improvement while helping them keep well-being intact. Include recommended reading.

A CAUTION

While AI can provide information on a wide range of topics, it does not "know" everything, especially highly specific topics not present in its training data. It can also give you inaccurate and nonsensical outcomes, a phenomenon commonly called a hallucination. Be aware of these limitations when seeking highly specialized or recent information (Shah, 2023).

The accuracy and relevance of responses from an AI chatbot can improve over time, though. You can expect general queries to be answered accurately, but for unique or specific school-related topics, a human touch or expertise is also required.

To get the best results, experiment with different AI platforms, and always confirm the information is accurate by cross-checking several websites or previewing the suggested books and journals. Consider factors such as credibility, authoritativeness, and how the information applies to your situation.

24. Launch Professional Learning Sessions

 **THE PROBLEM**

Agenda Abyss

"I love meetings," said no teacher, ever. And let's be honest, a meeting without an agenda makes it even worse—chaotic and aimless. Have you ever caught yourself daydreaming about lunch or mentally calculating how many minutes are left during a meeting? You're not alone; we have all been there. And when it is finally over, it resembles the bell ringing on the last day of school—pure relief.

When planning a professional learning session, think of the agenda as a teacher should think about a lesson plan. Forget to prepare one, and you've basically rolled out the red carpet for confusion and frustration.

 **THE SOLUTION**

Agenda Wizard

An AI assistant can take the stage as an Agenda Wizard. It has a remarkable ability to design an agenda to include all necessary topics—like magic. By using customized prompts, you ensure the agenda is both productive and beneficial. You'll also maximize your own time and effort. With a well-crafted agenda in hand, you will be able to guide sessions, promote engagement, and track progress with ease.

 **AN EXAMPLE**

The next example is a customizable template. Adjust the information to fit your situation.

This example aligns with ISTE Standard 3.5.d, Navigate Continuous Improvement, which states, "Develop the skills needed to lead and navigate change, advance systems and promote a mindset of continuous improvement for how technology can improve learning."

> Create an agenda for a professional learning session using the following information:
>
> WHO: Educators of a middle school faculty
>
> WHEN: Begin at 9 a.m. and end at noon.
>
> WHAT OBJECTIVES: 1) to understand and implement effective classroom management strategies, leading to a more conducive learning environment; 2) gain a comprehensive understanding of a new curriculum design.
>
> TOPICS TO INCLUDE: intro with icebreaker, best practices in classroom management, and curriculum design and planning.
>
> ADDITIONAL INFORMATION: Include time allotments for each segment. Allow for a 15-minute break.

 ACCELERATION

Professional learning can be designed in several ways. It does not always have to involve outside experts. Your own campus staff members can work wonders. So, nudge your teachers to explore new horizons and become leaders in the process. And for extra motivation, set up a system to reward their efforts. Let the AI chatbot show you how with this prompt providing suggested ways to let teachers take the lead. For more information on how to carry them out, just ask for more details on the model.

> List various models of professional learning that enlist teachers to lead learning sessions for their colleagues. Offer suggestions on how to incentivize and reward their participation.

25. Design Interactive Group Work

 THE PROBLEM

Design Dilemma

When designing professional learning, interactive group work is a must. Working with others has loads of benefits, but group work can be tricky to pull off. It may be tempting to skip it. But avoiding group work can result in many missed opportunities, leaving everyone in the dark.

 **THE SOLUTION**

Interactive Sparks

Enlist your AI assistant to help spark the interaction. Collaborative activities can warm up the crowd by encouraging active participation, critical thinking, and creating space for diverse perspectives.

Provide key information in the prompt such as the topic and title of the session. Define the audience and any important instructions. Try incorporating scenarios customized for your situation. Or, you can start by asking for suggestions on objectives, materials, and group activities.

 AN EXAMPLE

In this example, the prompt asks for small-group interaction. It also requests customized scenarios tailored to the specific campus or school setting. Customization is key to a meaningful activity.

 Provide an interactive small group activity focused on [insert topic, e.g., classroom management] for teachers of students in [insert grade level, e.g., grades 3 through 6]. The activity should align with the following objective [insert objective, e.g., to understand and implement effective classroom management strategies, leading to a more conducive learning environment].

Write three short scenarios that could be read and studied during group work. The scenarios will depict realistic situations that may occur in the classroom, such as [insert examples, e.g., student misbehavior and conflicts between students]. List possible responses to each scenario that represent best practices and ideas for discussion. List materials needed.

This example aligns with ISTE Standard 3.5.d, Navigate Continuous Improvement, which states, "Develop the skills needed to lead and navigate change, advance systems and promote a mindset of continuous improvement for how technology can improve learning."

 ACCELERATION

Inclusive group activities ensure all participants have an equal opportunity to contribute. The following prompt generates suggestions to meet this goal.

Act as the leader of a group of educators. Your goal is to foster collaboration, communication, and teamwork among them to enhance learning. Provide a list of effective strategies to achieve this goal, along with specific examples and implementation ideas. Include directions to encourage equal opportunity to contribute and foster teamwork among educators. Explain how each strategy can be implemented. Provide examples.

Specific Protocols

The following prompts focus on specific protocols to try out.

GAMIFICATION

Create a game based on "Who Wants to be a Millionaire". Create the content for a slide deck of 15 slides to play the game with a large group. Include 4 multiple choice answers with one correct answer relevant for teachers. Each slide should contain one question with four choices. Focus the game on reviewing the topic of [insert topic, e.g., T-TESS, the Texas recommended appraisal process]. Include any suggestions on how best to play the game.

COOPERATIVE LEARNING

Create an activity for small groups of teachers using cooperative learning to better understand [insert topic, e.g., reviewing new curriculum]. Include an explanation of the protocol guidelines and additional tips.

BRAINSTORMING

Design a brainstorming session. Present a situation for teachers of students in [insert details e.g., grade level, topic]. Include ways to think creatively and to document ideas generated by the group to learn [insert topic, e.g., calm down areas for student regulation]. Include an explanation of the protocol guidelines and additional tips.

JIGSAW

Create a jigsaw activity for small groups, giving each member a different task to learn about [insert topic, e.g., student engagement]. Include an explanation of the protocol guidelines.

ROLE PLAY

 Role play allows participants to try out an experience. Create an activity for a group of educators to learn best practices for [insert topic, e.g., parent conferences or ARD meetings]. Include an explanation of the protocol guidelines and additional tips.

PROBLEM SOLVING

 Set up an activity to include a scenario with a problem to be solved about [insert topic, e.g., student transitions in a kindergarten classroom]. The participants find solutions guided by a facilitator. Include an explanation of the protocol guidelines and additional tips.

TEAM COMPETITION

 Create an activity for a group of educators to use a team competition to learn more about [insert topic, e.g., classroom management]. Include an explanation of the protocol guidelines and additional tips.

CASE STUDY

 Create an activity using a case study about [insert topic, e.g., trauma-informed practices]. Write the case study using these details [insert details]. Invite participants to discuss questions and apply critical thinking about how to respond to the case. Include an explanation of the protocol guidelines and additional tips.

 A CAUTION

As with any response from your AI assistant, be sure to review the content provided by the machine. Most of these activities provide for open-ended responses, but when asking for specific answers in an activity, such as a game that has one right answer, be sure to verify answers with additional resources.

26. Generate Ideas for a Book Study

 THE PROBLEM

Bookish Blues

A faculty book study is a great way to learn new ideas, but it can have you singing the blues. Some pesky issues might pop up as you plan the experience. You'll need to find the right resources, get everyone engaged, and juggle conflicting schedules. Planning the book study on your own may leave you feeling overwhelmed and on the verge of hitting a sour note.

 THE SOLUTION

Literary Lifesaver

Using an AI assistant will have you singing a different tune. The chatbot can offer tips for organization, ideas for engagement and more. Enlist your AI thought partner in providing practical suggestions and actionable strategies. The collaboration will result in a memorable book study, which hits all the right notes in no time at all.

 AN EXAMPLE

The prompt below was created for a study about a great book entitled *Beyond Behaviors* by Mona Delahooke (2019). The book study presents a valuable opportunity for educators to engage in reflective learning. The book delves into the emotional and behavioral needs of students, offering insights that can significantly improve classroom practices. Through reflection, educators can analyze their current understanding of student behavior and identify areas for growth.

> " Create a summary and an outline for a book study with a group of educators about the book "Beyond Behaviors" by Dr. Mona Delahooke.

This example aligns with ISTE Standard 3.5.c, Engage in Reflective Practice, which states, "Use technology to regularly engage in reflective practices that support personal and professional growth."

 **ACCELERATION**

Try using the AI assistant for every aspect of the book study. The following prompts serve as a follow-up to the conversation. Add them to the same stream to get more results on the same topic or title. The process easily adapts to any book your team wants to study together. Enjoy.

Establish Goals and Objectives

 Create a goal for our book study and a list of objectives. Target key points of this book.

Plan the Schedule

 Generate a schedule for our book study. Include meeting dates [insert start and ending dates], times [insert start and ending time], and location [insert location]. Set realistic deadlines for the book study, considering the length of the book, the pace of reading, and the frequency of meetings or discussions.

Organize Logistics

 Design an agenda for each session. Include the goal, objectives, meeting date, chapter reading, and suggested questions for the book study.

Facilitate Discussions

 Generate interesting questions to guide discussions about the book. Design the questions for faculty members to think critically about the book's content and apply its concepts to their teaching practices.

Provide Additional Resources

 Generate a list of additional resources about the topic of this book. Include supplementary readings, videos, or online discussions for faculty members to deepen their understanding of the book's content.

Assess and Celebrate Progress

 Design an exercise for the book study group to summarize their takeaway from the author.

 Create a survey to gather feedback from faculty members on the effectiveness of the book study, which can be used to improve future book studies.

Celebrate Success

 Suggest ways to celebrate the book study's success by highlighting faculty members' accomplishments and acknowledging their dedication and contributions.

Choose your next book with an AI summary

 Write a one-paragraph summary of the book [insert title and author]. List the top five interesting aspects of the book.

 **A CAUTION**

Another reminder: AI assistants can get it wrong and be prone to hallucinations. So, it is important to carefully review and cross-check information with other sources.

27. Create a Checklist for the Start of School

 THE PROBLEM

Stumped at the Start

Transitioning into a new role or starting a new job can be challenging. There's a lot to learn, and staying organized and completing all essential tasks before the start date can get a little overwhelming. Your to-do list may involve making time to learn about the context, culture, and curriculum of the new role. With so many responsibilities and so little time, how do you keep it all straight?

THE SOLUTION

The Checklist Champion

Whether you're a newbie or a seasoned leader, a checklist is an excellent road map for your next project or the start of school. Checklists have always helped me prioritize and ensure no task gets overlooked. This simple tool will make any transition smoother. And there's no need to start with a blank page—let AI step up to help you master the art of organization.

When crafting the prompt, specify your role, job title, and experience level. This information will generate a checklist that meets your specific needs and challenges. Include information that focuses on the urgent and important tasks first so you can finish them on time. And include any particular focus areas, such as learning a specific curriculum or setting up local procedures.

AN EXAMPLE

This example would have been so helpful when I got a job in July and was preparing to start school in August. I could have leveraged AI's ability to spell out the vital tasks I needed to do before the school bell rang for the new year on a new school campus.

 I am a new campus principal for a campus serving PK through 4th grade. Generate a checklist of top-priority actions to do before the first month of school. Include time to study the new curriculum on trauma-informed learning.

This example aligns with ISTE Standard 3.5.d, Navigate Continuous Improvement, which states, "Develop the skills needed to lead and navigate change, advance systems and promote a mindset of continuous improvement for how technology can improve learning."

ACCELERATION

Incorporate Expert Knowledge

Consider incorporating expert knowledge into the prompt before requesting the checklist. Start by gathering relevant articles and reports, or ask AI to help you with a list. Next, copy the pertinent sections of these resources and paste them into the AI assistant's prompt window. Request a summary to have the AI distill the key insights from the content. Using this approach, you can efficiently extract and apply expert advice in the checklist. Notice the prompt uses a framework mentioned earlier.

> I have collected several articles, reports, and studies on advice for starting the school year and would like to understand the expert advice contained within them. Below, I have pasted relevant sections from these sources. Summarize the key points and insights. This summary will help me craft a checklist to use when starting the school year as a new principal.

Now write a follow-up prompt in the same stream that references the article. Try using a prompt framework.

> PERSONA: A campus principal starting a new year on a campus with 500 students in seventh through ninth grade.
>
> REQUEST: Using the actions from the previous information you summarized, generate a checklist of top-priority actions I need to do before the first day of school.
>
> OUTPUT: Add any other ideas or suggestions related to my situation to complete a comprehensive checklist for the start of school.

A Step-By-Step Tutorial

If you prefer a step-by-step tutorial, then try this prompt. This type of prompt can be adapted to learn almost anything. Try it out with anything you are ready to learn.

> Provide me with step-by-step instructions, in checklist form, on how to start the school year as the new principal of a Head Start PK campus.

Onboarding Employees

Try out a prompt to generate a checklist for onboarding new teachers.

> Create a checklist of the top priorities for new teachers beginning their first year at our elementary school. Include reminders of self-care.

28. Introduce AI to Teachers

 **THE PROBLEM**

Bulging Burdens

Teachers face an overwhelming number of administrative tasks, which can keep them from focusing on the many needs of their students. Occupied with lesson plans, grading, and other tasks, they often have little time left for actual teaching.

It is no wonder so many teachers feel burned out. They juggle a never-ending list of tasks and often feel as if they are not doing enough for their students. This can lead to major stress, anxiety, and even depression. School leaders need to find a way to reduce the bulging burden on teachers so they can focus on what they do best: teaching.

 **THE SOLUTION**

Task Transformation

By automating routine tasks and providing support, AI has the potential to transform the way we work. AI tools save time and can give teachers more time to focus on nurturing student growth and fostering success. Forward-thinking leaders must get in front of this new technology and use a proactive approach. This means looking for ways to use this tool rather than dismissing it as a new fad. AI has the capacity to enhance instruction—and transform the way we use and understand information.

Some teachers show an interest in using AI tools. The rollout has prompted both excitement and apprehension about its potential impact on the future of education. So, the first step leaders must take is to provide time and training to learn these new tools. But changes are best made through coaching, not through compliance and control.

Begin by providing an optional PD session for those interested in learning and sharing how AI works. Start small and give options. Don't try to implement AI all at once for everyone on campus. Start with a small group and a few small projects, and then scale up your efforts incrementally. This will help with buy-in from teachers and avoid overwhelming them.

During the session, invite teachers to discuss reactions and routine tasks they often encounter. Explore and discuss ideas on how AI can assist. And emphasize they do not need to worry about this tool taking over their jobs. A robot could never appreciate the fine art of managing a classroom during the chaos of a surprise fire drill.

AN EXAMPLE

You can explore AI with thought-provoking questions. The prompt will help generate those questions, which foster conversation. The aim is to build understanding by beginning with common ground.

> Create a set of questions about using AI in the classroom to use in a discussion session with teachers. Ensure chosen questions foster inclusivity, empathy, and meaningful dialogue.

This example aligns with ISTE Standard 3.5.d, Navigate Continuous Improvement, which states, "Develop the skills needed to lead and navigate change, advance systems and promote a mindset of continuous improvement for how technology can improve learning."

ACCELERATION

Incorporate an AI experiment into a teaching session. Help teachers generate samples from different prompts related to their work. Start by giving teachers a few different prompts related to their work. Have them use the AI to generate samples from these prompts. Then, discuss the results of the experiment and how to use AI in the classroom. Let the AI come up with suggestions for you to choose from for the activity.

> Create a list of simple prompts that are useful for teachers when they are first learning how to use an AI assistant. Focus the topics on administrative tasks, such as creating an email response, writing a social media post, or simply asking questions.

A CAUTION

AI has the potential to revolutionize education. But be cautious about how you use this technology. It is important to be transparent about how it works and what AI can do. Rather than fear AI, we can look at it as an opportunity. With careful planning and thoughtful use, AI can be a powerful tool for productivity, learning, and growth.

29. Facilitate Feedback on Lesson Plans

 THE PROBLEM

A Feedback Gap

There was a time when I naively thought spending hours alone in my office reviewing meticulously crafted lesson plans was the epitome of effective teacher oversight. But in reality, it felt like a checkbox exercise. Making teachers hand them in didn't necessarily translate to improved effectiveness or a more reflective, adventurous approach to teaching. While I'm a firm believer in a well-crafted lesson plan, this traditional method is undeniably time-consuming. It requires careful analysis and consideration, qualities often sacrificed under the weight of endless paperwork.

 THE SOLUTION

Lesson Plan Leverage

This is where AI can be a game changer. Using AI to provide feedback on a lesson plan can be a powerful tool to promote reflective practice for both teachers and supervisors. Instead of a traditional closed-door review, envision a collaborative process where teachers and the AI chatbot work together. The AI can analyze the lesson plan, identifying areas of strength and opportunities for improvement based on predefined criteria. It can then present its feedback in a clear and actionable way. This prompts the teacher to engage in critical reflection, considering the AI's suggestions and tailoring the lesson plan accordingly.

 AN EXAMPLE

Getting feedback from AI is as simple as copying and pasting a lesson plan into the AI assistant platform. Then, ask it a few questions, such as ways to improve or differentiate.

 Suggest ways to improve this lesson plan. Give me specific feedback. [Insert the lesson plan into the prompt].

This example aligns with ISTE Standard 3.3.a, Empower Educators, which states, "Empower educators to exercise professional agency, build teacher leadership skills and pursue personalized professional learning."

ACCELERATION

The conversation with the AI chatbot can continue by asking it to rewrite, revise, or add new elements.

> Using your suggestions, rewrite the lesson plan incorporating the suggestions and adding elements such as materials and assessment.

Occasionally, students or a whole class may need special help or adjustments. Provide details of any specific help needed for students with special needs. This helps the AI assistant provide specific and relevant feedback.

> A student in my class has a hearing impairment. Suggest specific interventions for this student during the following lesson: [insert copy of lesson plan].

30. Show Support for Student Mental Health

 THE PROBLEM

Post-Pandemic Mental Health Concerns

In the post-COVID 19 era, many students face significant mental health challenges, including feelings of isolation and loneliness, with an alarming rise in suicidal ideation across America. These challenges persist, underscoring the urgent need for integrating innovative teaching methodologies and cutting-edge research on mental health support for students.

 THE SOLUTION

AI-Powered Support

AI has the potential to significantly improve support for mental health intervention in schools. As highlighted in an EdSurge article (LaHayne, 2023), proactive mental health resources are crucial for all students, particularly adolescents. Research suggests the combination of emotional intelligence (EQ) and AI can be particularly effective in addressing the complexities of student needs, leading to greater academic success (Fullan & Matsuda, 2024). Use the following examples to further assist your search for actionable strategies to add to your strategic plan for supporting adolescent mental health.

 **AN EXAMPLE**

These examples offer ways to find and use resources to inform a strategic plan.

 I'm looking for online resources about supporting the mental health of [elementary/middle/high school] students in a post-COVID world.

After locating reputable evidence-based research and articles online, copy and paste portions into the prompt below. AI can use the summary to give your leadership team strategies and action steps to support students who need mental health support.

 I have collected information on the topic of post-COVID support for student mental health and would like a summary of the expert advice. [Copy and paste relevant information into the prompt].

After AI provides the summaries, use the following prompt in the same stream.

 Now use the information from the summaries to compile a list of suggested actions our campus can take to accomplish our goal of meeting the needs of our students, [insert goal(s)].

This example aligns with ISTE Standard 3.3.d, Use Tech to Meet Student Learning Needs, which states, "Support educators in using technology to advance learning that meets the diverse learning, cultural and social-emotional needs of individual students."

31. Prepare for Your Own Job Interview

 THE PROBLEM

Job Application Jitters

Creating a personalized resume and cover letter for a job application can take a while. It can also feel stressful, particularly when exploring many job options.

Customizing each application requires careful attention to detail. This involves researching the company and aligning your skills and experiences with what they're looking for in the role. The time and effort involved in customizing each application can add up, leading to high stress levels. You must meet deadlines while maintaining the quality of your application materials.

The repetitive nature of the task can be a drag. It can lead to fatigue and a lack of motivation, which can impact the application quality.

 THE SOLUTION

The Resume Remodeler

If you're currently job hunting, the AI assistant has got your back. You can use it to quickly tailor each application for the job posting. Then, you can ask AI for help with your resume. It can suggest changes to the content, fonts, headers, and bullets. (But don't let it get too carried away, or you might end up sounding like a Nobel Prize winner.) Save time and reduce stress on your job-hunting journey.

 AN EXAMPLE

The AI assistant helps review and suggest revisions to resume content. You can include only part of the resume or the entire document in the prompt.

 Review the education section of my resume and provide constructive feedback on how to improve it. Make suggestions for revising the content and formatting to highlight my academic achievements, skills, and relevant coursework clearly and concisely. Feedback needs to be specific and actionable, providing concrete suggestions. Ensure the language is easy to understand while conveying the necessary information to potential employers. Provide guidance on how to place and format the education section within the overall structure of the resume. [Copy and paste resume into the prompt].

This example illustrates ISTE Standard 3.5.a, Stay Current on Innovation in Learning, which states, "Set goals to remain current on emerging technologies for learning, innovations in pedagogy and advancements in the learning sciences."

 ACCELERATION

Preparing for the interview is also a great time to use the AI assistant. Include the job description and any other relevant information about the potential employers.

Suggest questions I may be asked during an interview for the role of Assistant Principal at [name of campus]. And offer tips for a successful interview.

If you need assistance with responding to common job interview questions, just ask the chatbot. For instance, you might prompt the AI assistant this way.

When responding to questions during an interview,

Suggest ways to highlight my relevant experience and skills [insert details].

Provide suggestions for how to deal with difficult situations or challenges occurring on a school campus.

And outline ways to discuss my career goals and aspirations [insert details].

If you're unsure about what is and is not appropriate to ask in a particular interview setting, ask. The AI assistant can also provide information on common interview etiquette. It can offer tips for how to avoid common pitfalls and make a positive impression on a potential employer. Try out this prompt to find out what not to ask.

When interviewing for a job as a [insert role, e.g., new principal], what questions should I NOT ask? Explain common interview etiquette and any other common pitfalls to avoid.

After the interview, let AI help you write a personalized letter of thanks to the interview committee.

Write a sincere and thoughtful letter of thanks to the [name] school district interview committee. The letter needs to express appreciation for their time, effort, and consideration. Include details about my positive, professional, and interesting interview experience. Aim to make a meaningful connection. Add any details or anecdotes to enhance the letter, such as [insert anecdotes]. Highlight my enthusiasm for joining their school district.

Let's say you're offered the job. Congratulations. Now you may want to negotiate the salary, but this can be a tricky conversation. Let the AI assistant roleplay a salary negotiation with you. To make this scenario as realistic and helpful as possible, provide the chatbot with some details.

> Role-play a negotiation with me using the following information. Provide suggestions for effective responses and give me examples of how to craft my answers.
>
> 1. The position I am negotiating for is [insert job title].
> 2. The salary I hope to secure in this negotiation is [insert range of amount].
> 3. Specific points I expect the employer to raise are [insert concerns].
> 4. Some non-salary benefits or terms important in this negotiation are [insert items, e.g., health insurance, vacation time, substitute support].

32. Jazz Up Your LinkedIn Profile

THE PROBLEM

Profile Predicament

A well-crafted LinkedIn profile is a powerful tool for professional success, but many people struggle to translate their skills and experience into a compelling narrative that grabs the attention of recruiters and potential employers.

THE SOLUTION

AI-Enhanced Branding

Investing time crafting a compelling narrative doesn't just improve your profile; it positions you as a proactive professional who understands how to effectively market your skills and value in today's competitive job market. But if you're looking for a new job, transform your profile into a compelling narrative with the help of AI. You may attract recruiters and potential employers looking for the perfect fit.

AN EXAMPLE

This example aligns with ISTE Standard 3.5.a, Stay Current on Innovation in Learning, which states, "Set goals to remain current on emerging technologies for learning, innovations in pedagogy and advancements in the learning sciences."

My LinkedIn profile looks more like a static resume and less like a dynamic showcase of my leadership potential. I'm a passionate school leader with [number] years of experience fostering a positive learning environment for students. My focus on [leadership value 1] and [leadership value 2] has led to successful initiatives in [mention achievement/program]. I'm particularly excited about [future of education focus] and connecting with other education professionals on LinkedIn to share best practices and collaborate on innovative projects. Using this information, write a new profile for my online presence.

33. Learn How to Manage Your Health

 THE PROBLEM

A Light That's Nearly Out

Educators are some of the most overworked and stressed-out professionals. We're always trying to balance work, family, and personal life. And if not careful, the lights can dim—or burn out.

When I first became an administrator, I was excited and very engrossed in the role. I wanted to dedicate every minute to my new job. I found myself skipping lunch and resorting to fast food on my way home. Obviously, I didn't understand the value of self-care. I would work late hours, arrive early, and carry the weight of my frustrations and extra work home with me. I pushed myself to the limit, and it was a recipe for stress. I pay for it now with a daily dose of blood pressure medication—a lesson learned the hard way.

 THE SOLUTION

Stress-Busting Suggestions

If you feel stressed, your AI chatbot can help you with suggestions and reminders about how to relax and take better care of yourself. We know how to stay healthy, but sometimes we need help getting back on track.

 AN EXAMPLE

Enlist the AI chatbot as your personal coach for well-being. The brain can respond to all kinds of reinforcements and reminders, even if the words are from a robot.

> I am stressed out. Suggest five clear and concise strategies to help me reduce anxiety symptoms and promote a sense of calm and relaxation. I want to learn to keep my eye on the big picture and not overinvest in the small stuff.

> How does the vagus nerve affect stress and learning? How can I calm this nerve?

This example aligns with ISTE Standard 3.5.a, Stay Current on Innovation in Learning, which states, "Set goals to remain current on emerging technologies for learning, innovations in pedagogy and advancements in the learning sciences."

ACCELERATION

Consider using AI as your health coach to achieve your personal health goals.

> I want to learn a new habit of eating more nutritious meals and not skipping lunch during work. My schedule allows for a 20-minute lunch each day at 1 p.m., so I also need to plan for a low-sugar snack mid-morning. I will know I've reached my goal if I am consistent. Write a SMARTIE goal for healthy eating habits. Explain how this goal is essential for my health and add any additional tips to help me learn this new habit.

AI assistants can create personalized meal plans to match your preferences and dietary requirements. They can also help you create a balanced menu or give you snack ideas by customizing suggestions. (Too bad it can't prepare the meals too—at least not yet.)

> Design a weekly lunch menu for a busy professional. Make it nutritious, easy to prepare, and [insert personal preferences].

> Tabulate snack ideas that contain high nutrition and low sugar.

A CAUTION

The training process for AI machines involves a wide variety of text from different sources, including reputable organizations such as the American Psychological Association. But generated responses come from statistical patterns, so they might not always be accurate or reliable. To make sure the information is accurate, verify what the AI tool provides with other sources.

- Look for other sources to corroborate the information.
- Use your judgment. If something does not seem right, it probably isn't.

Discussion Questions: Personalized Professional Learning

Using AI for professional growth offers endless possibilities. Take some time to discuss what you and your team have learned about the role of AI in personalized professional learning. The discussions will not only deepen your understanding but also enhance your team's approach to teaching and learning.

1. How do you currently approach personalized professional learning for yourself and your team? In what ways does or could AI tech factor in?

2. Have you utilized AI to suggest feedback on lesson plans? If yes, what was the outcome? How did it improve the quality of lesson planning and delivery?

3. How does AI help you keep up with the newest educational trends and teaching methods? How have you used AI-recommended resources or best practices?

4. Have you explored using AI to assist with writing skills or to write interventions for students? If yes, what were the outcomes?

5. Have you encountered any issues when using AI for professional growth? How have you addressed or overcome them?

6. AI can generate outlines for book studies—have you tried it? If yes, what was the impact? How did it assist in organizing and facilitating meaningful book study discussions?

7. What other ways could you use AI to help professionals grow or make classroom tasks easier?

Chapter 6

DATA MANAGEMENT AND SCHOOL IMPROVEMENT

AS A FIRST-YEAR PRINCIPAL leading a campus of 400 kindergarten and pre-K students, intuition was my guidepost. One of the first issues I tackled was how the students used computers. Most teachers felt the structured lab environment was better suited for these young learners. But whispers of discontent arose when I proposed breaking up the lab and moving the computers to classroom stations. A nagging doubt persisted: Was this truly best for the students?

To answer that question, we turned to data. We tracked computer usage from classrooms who agreed to try the stations and those who worked in the lab. The results surprised me. While classroom stations fostered basic digital literacy skills, they lacked the focus and engaging software of the dedicated lab. This data exposed a blind spot in my intuition. Armed with this newfound clarity, we collaborated to revamp the lab with even more engaging software and incorporated focused lab sessions into the curriculum.

This experience informed and shaped my approach to leadership. It revealed the limitations of intuition and the power of data-driven decision-making. Data became the compass for continuous improvement, guiding our program forward. I often wonder what it would have been like to have had the advantage of AI when I was getting started.

In chapter 6, we dive into the world of data management and school improvement with the help of AI. You will explore how AI tools provide tailored strategies for school leaders to effectively leverage data to improve conditions within your school system. Examples in this chapter align with Education Leader Standard 3.4, System Designer. This standard has four key areas of focus. You will also find examples from Standard 3.2 Visionary Planner: Engaging in strategic planning and fostering a shared vision for the effective use of technology in teaching and learning.

Connection to the ISTE Standards for Leaders

3.4 Systems Designer
Leaders build teams and systems to implement, sustain and continually improve the use of technology to support learning.

3.4.a Lead teams to collaboratively establish the robust infrastructure and systems needed to implement the strategic plan.

3.4.b Ensure that resources for supporting the effective use of technology for learning are sufficient and scalable to meet future demand.

3.4.c Protect privacy and security by ensuring that students and staff observe effective privacy and data management policies.

3.4.d Establish partnerships that support the strategic vision, achieve learning priorities and improve operations.

34. Use Data to Monitor and Improve Conditions

THE PROBLEM

Data Dilemmas

In my experience, good schools constantly gather information on everything from student conduct and safety to teacher and parent satisfaction. But let's face it, this data can easily become a burden without the right tools. It ends up piling high, gathering dust, and its potential goes untapped.

THE SOLUTION

Data-Driven Decisions

The good news? Powerful AI tools are emerging that can unlock the true potential of this data. By harnessing its power, schools can transform this raw data into actionable insights to inform decisions and drive real change, ultimately creating a more positive learning environment for everyone.

AN EXAMPLE

Let AI provide suggestions and ways to use data to help your leadership team evaluate progress, make course corrections, and measure impact to make positive changes within your school community.

> Our district leadership team is looking for ways to use data effectively to evaluate progress on this goal: [insert goal, e.g., Improve culture and wellness in our school community among the adults on campus]. Offer suggestions and provide examples for how to make course corrections and measure impact.

This example aligns closely with the ISTE Standard 3.2.c, Create a Shared Vision, which states, "Evaluate progress on the strategic plan, make course corrections, measure impact and scale effective approaches for using technology to transform learning."

ACCELERATION

Get more specific by drilling down with the Plan-Do-Study-Act framework.

> Help our school leadership team use the Plan-Do-Study-Act (PDSA) framework to improve [insert topic or goal, e.g., educator wellness on campus]. What data will we need to collect to measure impact? Give us five examples.

A CAUTION

Data may seem objective—but it is not. It reflects the priorities and limitations of the people collecting, analyzing, and using it. People decide what information to gather, how to structure it, and what narratives to extract. This injects subjectivity, bias, and blind spots into the results. Recognizing the human fingerprints on data and guarding against unconscious bias are vital steps to data management (McIntosh and Rowly, 2021).

When you enter data for analysis, prioritize privacy protection and follow data security protocols to keep sensitive information safe.

35. Launch a Culture Audit

 THE PROBLEM

Sound the Siren

I once stepped into a new job as the principal at a campus that had just lost its previous leader under problematic circumstances. The campus was struggling and felt much like a person with a grave illness. Traditional challenges like one-size-fits-all assessments and inadequate funding certainly hinder progress, but the root cause can also lie deeper—in a disjointed school culture. A school's culture is the bedrock of student learning. Just like a doctor needs health data to prescribe a remedy, I realized we needed a comprehensive look at the school's well-being. Navigating these challenges was tough as a new leader. And back then I didn't have AI technology, so it took quite a bit of time.

 THE SOLUTION

Audit for Answers

AI technology offers a powerful solution to rebuild a struggling school culture by assisting with a culture audit. Imagine having a high-tech ally that analyzes surveys and feedback, pinpointing areas for improvement and uncovering underlying concerns. This frees up valuable time to focus on understanding the campus's needs, paving the way to design actions that meet those needs. AI empowers us to make informed decisions based on real data that foster a thriving learning community where exploration and student success flourish.

 AN EXAMPLE

This prompt starts a conversation with AI about what to focus on in a culture audit.

> You are a member of a leadership team at a neighborhood school. List the topics to consider for a campus culture audit. Then, ask us questions to help us get started. Our goal is to create an assessment or audit that provides a personalized, actionable view of student progress in real time.

These examples align with ISTE Standard 3.2.d, Communicate with Stakeholders, which states, "Communicate effectively with stakeholders to gather input on the plan, celebrate successes and engage in a continuous improvement cycle."

ACCELERATION

After narrowing the audit's focus to a critical topic, use the AI to create questions for a survey.

> Create a survey for [insert audience, e.g., faculty, students, or parents] with no more than 5 open-ended questions. Focus on this topic: [insert 1 topic, e.g., staff well-being]. Design the survey to include both closed and open-ended questions.

Then you're ready to enlist the AI to analyze the data.

> Using the data provided, analyze the responses to inform the campus culture audit. Identify hidden patterns, areas of improvement, and opportunities for positive change within our school community. [insert the open-ended responses from surveys].

36. Generate a Faculty Survey

 THE PROBLEM

Feedback Fiasco

The art of gathering effective feedback involves a balancing act. While brevity is key, you also need enough detail to make it actionable. Crafting unbiased, anonymous questions is crucial, but the practicalities of distributing and collecting surveys add another layer. Striking the right balance to capture everyone's perspective in a single survey can be challenging.

 THE SOLUTION

Survey Success

Unlock the power of AI to whip up a savvy survey. The process takes finesse, but quality feedback is worth the effort. With AI's help, the survey can be tailored to your campus needs. With its magic, you can come up with questions that are right on the mark. Once you have gathered all the necessary information, it can quickly and efficiently analyze and report what you've found. You will be able to make smart decisions and keep everyone on track. No more headaches, just straight-up solutions.

AN EXAMPLE

This prompt focuses on creating a survey with a specific focus.

> Generate a list of five open-ended survey questions for the school faculty. The purpose of the survey is to collect perspectives on campus needs and wants, focused on [insert goals, e.g., fostering a sense of community and well-being].

These examples align with ISTE Standard 3.2.d, Communicate with Stakeholders, which states, "Communicate effectively with stakeholders to gather input on the plan, celebrate successes and engage in a continuous improvement cycle."

 ACCELERATION

If you want a quick overview or an in-depth exploration of how to use surveys, AI is ready to go. Let it explain the many ways you can use surveys for campus improvement.

> Create a list of ways I can use a digital survey, such as Google Forms, in our school to improve [insert focus area, e.g., the well-being of the adults who work here].

37. Generate a Student Survey

 THE PROBLEM

A Tricky Dilemma

One way to understand school issues is to give students a voice through a survey or focus group. But creating questions, analyzing responses, and summarizing results takes a lot of time.

 THE SOLUTION

Fast Track Feedback

AI can streamline the process of collecting student feedback. AI-powered platforms can automatically generate questions, analyze responses, and summarize results. This can save leadership teams valuable time and resources while still giving them access to the feedback they need to improve student engagement.

AN EXAMPLE

In this example, the AI assists in creating survey questions for older students.

 Create five survey questions for students that are clear, specific, relevant, and inclusive. The purpose of the survey is to give students a voice on issues affecting them in school. Use a combination of open- and closed-ended questions. Write in a casual style at a reading level for students in [insert grade level, e.g., 10th through 12th grade].

These examples align with ISTE Standard 3.2.d, Communicate with Stakeholders, which states, "Communicate effectively with stakeholders to gather input on the plan, celebrate successes and engage in a continuous improvement cycle."

ACCELERATION

Some students may struggle to understand complex language and sentence structures, making it difficult for them to comprehend and respond to survey questions. One solution to overcome this challenge is to prompt AI to adapt the questions to suit the age and language proficiency of students. In the following prompt, the questions are adapted by reading level.

 Write five more questionswith a reading level of [insert level, e.g., second-grade]

38. Analyze an Open-Ended Questionnaire

THE PROBLEM

Drowning in Data

Open-ended questions capture answers that show how people think. But manually analyzing large amounts of open-ended data is time-consuming and challenging. It can leave you drowning in data. Likert scale questions (rate from 1 to 5) are often the go-to because of their simplicity and speed. But they don't capture the full spectrum of human sentiment.

 **THE SOLUTION**

Smooth Sailing

AI can help solve this problem by streamlining the process. With AI's support, data analysis is smooth sailing. Michael Gaskell, a principal in New Jersey working at Hammarskjold Upper Elementary School in New Jersey, uses AI to get feedback on open-ended questions. "School leaders are busy individuals who need important and accurate information quickly so they can act on it. This new method allows the school leader to do what is most important: share the feedback with stakeholders and act on it" (2023).

 AN EXAMPLE

This prompt helps find themes and patterns in open-ended responses, which can reveal areas for improvement and targeted interventions.

> Analyze these open-ended responses from a survey designed to assess perceptions of [insert target audience, e.g., students, teachers]. Note common themes, positive and negative responses, and any suggestions in the comments.
>
> Participants were asked: [insert questions].
>
> The responses included these comments: [insert comments].

These examples align with ISTE Standard 3.2.d, Communicate with Stakeholders, which states, "Communicate effectively with stakeholders to gather input on the plan, celebrate successes and engage in a continuous improvement cycle."

 A CAUTION

Remember NOT to share any sensitive information in the prompt that could compromise privacy or security, such as names, email addresses, or any identifying information.

39. Use Student Feedback to Motivate or Modify

 THE PROBLEM

Lights, Camera, No Action

We've all encountered students who seem not to care and don't want to learn. Motivating unmotivated students can be a huge challenge. Looking back, I regret not using student feedback more often to address this issue. If I could offer one piece of advice to fellow leaders, it would be this: flip the switch for zoned-out students by including their ideas.

 THE SOLUTION

Students on Center Stage

After collecting student perspectives in a survey, try meshing the feedback with evidence-based strategies. Then use an AI assistant to connect ideas and generate creative suggestions. Harness the power of student insights with evidence-based ideas; find new ways to get students in the act.

 AN EXAMPLE

When creating the prompt, let the AI chatbot find specific statements about motivation from the student survey or focus group. This provides context for the AI assistant to generate relevant insights.

1. Review these student comments and find those reflecting a lack of motivation. [Insert comments and responses from the survey].

2. Using those comments, suggest ways to motivate students who report they are unmotivated and disengaged.

3. Incorporate strategies noted as best practices from motivation theory, along with the student comments in the response.

These examples align with ISTE Standard 3.2.d, Communicate with Stakeholders, which states, "Communicate effectively with stakeholders to gather input on the plan, celebrate successes and engage in a continuous improvement cycle."

ACCELERATION

Students who say they have trouble understanding the material are providing important feedback that can be used to differentiate instruction and scaffold learning. This requires giving different levels of support to students based on their individual needs and breaking down a complex task into smaller, more manageable steps. These interventions can help students understand the task and feel more confident in their ability to complete it. In this example, AI is prompted to provide a personalized learning experience for a student.

> You are a teacher who has assigned a task to a student who is struggling to understand the concept of [insert topic, e.g., photosynthesis]. Show a visual. Explain the concept with a reading level of [insert level, e.g., third grade].

This next prompt can generate the content for a slide presentation.

> You are a teacher of [insert grade level/subject, e.g., ninth-grade science] who has assigned a task. One student needs help understanding the concept of [insert topic, e.g., thermodynamics]. Create a narrated slideshow of images explaining the concept. Describe the images. Use Slide 1, Slide 2, etc. Explain the concept using a reading level of [insert grade level, e.g., 5th grade] with narration correlated to each slide.

40. Write a Job Description and Guidebook

THE PROBLEM

Job Description Juggles

Writing a job description is a tedious task. It requires careful consideration and attention to detail. The process involves analyzing, researching, writing, fine-tuning, and then repeating the entire process. Maintaining up-to-date and well-crafted job descriptions is a necessary evil, but it is also a drain on time and energy. If only there were a way to automate the process.

THE SOLUTION

Your Recruitment Sidekick

Your AI assistant can make this happen by streamlining the process in no time. It will provide suggestions, offer language options, and assist in generating well-structured and engaging job descriptions. You can design and refine the qualifications and responsibilities in minutes. Using AI is like having a personal assistant who never complains. This saves valuable time and helps you get on to the more important task of hiring the right people for your team.

AN EXAMPLE

When you need help writing a job description for a mentor of new teachers, the following prompt might work as a starting point. Keep asking the chatbot to refine it until it matches your needs.

> Our school district needs a job description for a mentor of new teachers. Write the description with engaging and appealing language for potential candidates. Identify key responsibilities, outline expectations, and highlight specific qualifications or certifications necessary for the role. The goal is to establish a robust infrastructure for hiring effective professionals.

These examples align with ISTE Standard 3.4.a, Establish Infrastructure & Systems, which states, "Lead teams to collaboratively establish the robust infrastructure and systems needed to implement the strategic plan."

ACCELERATION

When writing the prompt, try including keywords relevant to the job title. And if you need a list of possible keywords, of course ask the AI chatbot for that too.

> Create a job description for a [insert role, e.g., elementary school counselor] and include these keywords: [insert relevant terms, e.g., Conflict Resolution, Multi-tiered Intervention (MTI), Social-Emotional Learning (SEL), Crisis Prevention Intervention (CPI), Individual Education Plan (IEP), Student Advocacy, Restorative Circles, Group Therapy, Community Partnerships].

Job descriptions can serve as a starting point, but a guidebook for the position can illuminate the role in helpful ways. Let your AI assistant help you create a Quick Start Guide for almost any role on campus.

> Create a Quick Start Guide for a [insert role, e.g., elementary school secretary].
>
> Use this outline for the guidebook and add details: [insert outline topics and details, e.g., Introduction, Responsibilities, Emotional Intelligence, Confidentiality, Customer Service, Gatekeeping, Technology: Google Tools, Data Management, Proofreading, Questioning, Learning Styles, Resolving Conflict].

 **A CAUTION**

It is a good idea to have job descriptions reviewed by other experts, such as HR professionals or hiring managers. This will help ensure the job descriptions are accurate and effective.

41. Refine Procedures for a Smooth Year

 THE PROBLEM

The Headache of Faulty Procedures

I vividly remember my first year as an assistant principal. The common areas, like the cafeteria, halls, and playgrounds, buzzed with activity throughout the day. Students hurried between classes; lunches were a whirlwind of noise and movement. Managing the flow of people in these shared spaces felt challenging and stressful.

 THE SOLUTION

Unleash the Game Changer

AI empowers educators with a toolbox of data-driven solutions for managing common areas. These intelligent recommendations can streamline processes, optimize scheduling, and suggest effective protocols, ultimately improving the overall flow and safety in schools.

AN EXAMPLE

In this example, the campus wellness team is working toward creating a safer and more enjoyable playground experience for students while supporting overall well-being and balance in the school community.

> Our school campus is focused on promoting well-being for students and adults. We are seeing issues on the playground. These include: [Add details, e.g., students hurting others and teachers feeling stressed]. Share strategies for enhancing playground safety. Include ideas that align with our goal of creating safe and joyful learning environments.

This example aligns with ISTE Standard 3.4.a, Establish Infrastructure & Systems, which states, "Lead teams to collaboratively establish the robust infrastructure and systems needed to implement the strategic plan."

42. Design New Procedures for Cafeteria Monitoring

 THE PROBLEM

Cafeteria Conundrum

School cafeterias always presented a unique set of challenges for me. From ensuring a smooth flow of students during lunch to managing noise levels and fostering a welcoming environment, effective cafeteria management requires careful planning and strategy. Regular brainstorming and collaboration are essential for identifying specific procedures and strategies to create an optimal lunch experience for everyone. But I barely had time to eat trying to figure out this puzzle.

 THE SOLUTION

Lunchroom Brilliance

Instead of relying solely on intuition, AI can provide a leadership team with a wealth of data-driven insights for optimizing their cafeterias. AI can analyze factors like student preferences, noise levels, and traffic patterns to generate creative suggestions. These suggestions can spark discussions and collaborative efforts among staff, leading to the implementation of effective strategies for a calmer and more enjoyable lunch experience. Ultimately, this can contribute to a positive well-being for both students and staff, transforming the cafeteria into a welcoming and pleasant space.

 **AN EXAMPLE**

This example focuses on how to handle cafeteria noise in an elementary setting.

 Younger students are usually excited to talk to each other during lunch, and some of them want to play instead of eat. The noise level in the room can get overwhelming. Generate a set of procedures for managing the noise level in an elementary school cafeteria during lunch. Compose them so they are easy to explain to very young children.

These examples align with ISTE Standard 3.4.a, Establish Infrastructure & Systems, which states, "Lead teams to collaboratively establish the robust infrastructure and systems needed to implement the strategic plan."

 ACCELERATION

Try using AI to help with suggestions for other aspects, such as classroom transitions, scheduling a staggered lunch period, and managing transitions to after-lunch recess. Or brainstorm issues about open seating arrangements in middle or high school cafeterias.

In this example, the AI prompt asks for ideas to help older students feel included and valued during open-seated lunchtime. AI can offer many potential strategies and approaches to help students feel more connected and supported within the school community. These are customizable for any situation.

 The seating in our high school cafeteria is self-selected, so a student who does not have a group of friends may feel uncomfortable. What procedures or practices can we use with older students? We want them to feel included, not isolated, and learn social skills during lunch on a school campus.

 A CAUTION

AI can offer many great suggestions. It is essential, however, to discuss these suggestions with relevant stakeholders such as teachers, cafeteria staff, and students. These conversations can lead to solutions aligned with the school's unique environment and goals.

43. Reinforce Routines and Procedures

 THE PROBLEM

Restroom Rule Challenges

During my tenure as a principal, I encountered some unforgettable situations in school restrooms. When students neglect to follow the rules, often it is because they weren't adequately taught how to use the restroom properly. This is not merely about keeping spaces clean; it is about instilling a sense of respect and responsibility. Schools everywhere grapple with this.

 THE SOLUTION

Signage That Signals Success

So how can AI help with this? Involve students in the process of finding a solution. Start by introducing how an AI assistant can generate rules for a restroom. After it generates suggestions, invite the students to share their opinions and revisions. Then, get them to use the content to make reminder signs to hang on school restroom walls.

 AN EXAMPLE

In this example, the AI offers a list of rules to use on posters in school restrooms. If you have 10 students in the group, ask the AI assistant to write 10 rules so each student can make a poster.

> Generate a list of 10 rules to put on posters for the school restroom. The posters remind students of rules for using the school restrooms. These posters will hang in or near the restrooms. Write them in simple language and suggest images so non-readers can understand the message.

This example aligns with ISTE Standard 3.4.a Establish Infrastructure & Systems, which states, "Lead teams to collaboratively establish the robust infrastructure and systems needed to implement the strategic plan."

 ACCELERATION

AI can suggest more areas for rule reminders, such as cafeteria manners, hallway behavior, or playground safety. Students may draw their own pictures for the posters or enlist some AI tools to create images, including DALL•E and Canva. Also try using Gemini to find a picture illustrating the rule.

Create or find a picture to illustrate this rule: [insert rule, e.g., person washing their hands].

More ideas? Here is a template for a prompt to help school leaders design routines and procedures for other common processes on a school campus. Choose a topic and add details about the current issues and opportunities. Here are a few examples: Attendance and tardiness policies; Classroom participation and engagement; Homework and assignment submission; Test-taking and assessment procedures; Study skills and time management strategies; Peer collaboration and group work; Student behavior and disciplinary procedures; Extracurricular activities and clubs; Playground safety and scheduling ; Student leadership and involvement opportunities; Academic support services and tutoring programs; College and career guidance services; Student feedback and evaluation mechanisms; School communication channels with students; Transition procedures (e.g., new student orientation); Student well-being and mental health support resources.

 What procedures or practices can improve [insert topic] on our school campus?

 A CAUTION

Involving students, teachers, and stakeholders helps ensure that AI suggestions are effective. Working together and sharing ideas can help customize the reminders for each school. Also, review the AI suggestions to make sure they align with the school's rules and values.

44. Design Protocols Related to Safety Issues

 THE PROBLEM

Break-In Bewilderment
I remember getting calls in the middle of the night about an alarm going off at the school campus. It's a priority for school administrators to keep buildings safe and secure. However, break-ins happen, putting students, staff, and the learning environment at risk. Finding effective solutions for safety concerns and preventing future break-ins is crucial, but it can get complicated.

THE SOLUTION

Security Strongholds

AI helps leaders before and after problems arise. Before an issue, AI looks at past events to guess what might happen next and tests plans. After the issue, AI checks what went well or wrong and suggests ways to do better next time. AI suggestions can help leaders maintain smooth and safe operations.

 AN EXAMPLE

In this example, AI offers a list of actions to take after a break-in. A follow-up prompt might ask for ways to prevent future break-ins and improve building safety overall. Use the suggestions in a discussion with your school safety team.

> List important actions for a school leadership team to carry out after an illegal break-in at the school building. Include other safety measures to consider that will strengthen the infrastructure and systems needed to secure a safe learning environment.

This example aligns with ISTE Standard 3.4.a Establish Infrastructure & Systems, which states, "Lead teams to collaboratively establish the robust infrastructure and systems needed to implement the strategic plan."

 A CAUTION

To use AI suggestions for school safety, collaborate with school personnel and local authorities regarding best practices.

45. Revise the Wording of School Policy

 THE PROBLEM

A Policy Puzzle

Excitement bubbled in my stomach as I walked into my new office at the school. Fresh start, clean slate—all that jazz. But that enthusiasm sputtered when I spotted a mountain of dusty notebooks piled on the floor by my desk. They were filled with campus rules and schedules but felt more like a stack of accusatory warnings. Lines about "unauthorized absences exceeding …" and "dress code violations resulting in …" screamed from the pages. It was a far cry from a welcoming introduction, painting a picture of a staff perpetually on the verge of transgression.

Crafting or revising these policies, however, is no walk in the park. It requires careful consideration of the language used, the intended outcome, and even legal parameters. It took time, but I reworded each page; if only I'd had AI!

 ## THE SOLUTION

A Policy Makeover

Those dusty notebooks on the floor became a stark reminder: clear communication is key, and effective policies are more than just a list of rules; they're a foundation for a successful school community. AI can provide ideas on how to revise policy statements, such as rules about using personal and sick leave. It can clarify the writing, address potential ambiguities, and align with best practices. It will also help to balance individual needs while maintaining school operations.

In their book *Deepening Digital Citizenship*, Carrie Rogers-Whitehead and Vanessa Monterosa stress the importance of including different viewpoints to create and refine policy. "A policy that reflects stakeholder voices outlines the actions and behaviors we want to see from our community" (2023). A discussion of the suggestions for the handbook can help refine the policy statement to better meet needs. Everyone benefits when policy supports an effective and inclusive working environment.

 ## AN EXAMPLE

This example provides a template to prompt the AI assistant to make policy suggestions. It is a great starting point for a discussion of what the AI suggests.

 How would you revise this policy statement for our campus? Provide suggestions. [Insert policy statement]

In addition to feedback from those who will need to follow the policy, enlist AI to give your team suggestions. This example aligns with ISTE Standard 3.2.d, Communicate with Stakeholders, which states, "Communicate effectively with stakeholders to gather input on the plan, celebrate successes and engage in a continuous improvement cycle."

A CAUTION

The AI assistant can suggest ideas, but experts and advisors should review and improve the final policy. This ensures compliance with local regulations and considers the school's context and needs.

46. Summarize a Meeting

THE PROBLEM

Note Taking Nightmares

Taking detailed notes and summarizing a meeting can be draining, even for dedicated professionals. But if this task is ignored and the details from a meeting are not documented, it can lead to a host of challenges. "The faintest ink is more powerful than the strongest memory." This Chinese proverb reminds us that human memory can be unreliable. Without documentation, details can be forgotten and mistakes made. These oversights can foster misunderstandings, create accountability issues, and erode trust.

THE SOLUTION

A Samurai Summarizer

Your AI assistant revolutionizes documentation with the precision and discipline of the famed samurai of Japan. Instead of jotting down notes or key points from meetings, you can dictate or type the meeting details into a prompt. The AI creates a summary to share with others in the meeting. Digital assistants help organize information, highlight important details, and ensure nothing important is missed.

AI can generate a concise or elaborate report that captures the essential information from the meeting. The report can provide a bulleted or narrative-style summary, highlighting key discussions, decisions, and action points. This enables school educators to effectively communicate important updates, policies, procedures, or logistical information to the faculty and staff.

AN EXAMPLE

In the example below, the AI assistant helps document approval for a teacher to attend a conference. The format can be a memo, letter, or report.

> Write a memo from a campus administrator to a staff member confirming approval to attend an educational conference for professional learning. This memo follows a conversation regarding a request by the teacher to attend. Include a reminder to submit a substitute request. Add a reminder to send a copy of the printed certificate of completion to the office secretary. And encourage them to share information with colleagues upon return. Commend them for their ongoing learning pursuits.

These examples align with ISTE Standard 3.2.d, Communicate with Stakeholders, which states, "Communicate effectively with stakeholders to gather input on the plan, celebrate successes and engage in a continuous improvement cycle."

ACCELERATION

Get Help Summarizing a Meeting

AI can also transform large volumes of information seamlessly into succinct responses, ready to be inserted into your weekly newsletter.

> Convert these meeting notes into a narrative. Limit the report to 50 words that will be used in a newsletter to campus staff. Change the short-hand notes into a first-hand account of the meeting. Include this information and commend the team for their great work.
>
> Date and time:
>
> Number and names of people present:
>
> Leader of the meeting:
>
> Notes:

Get Help Transcribing an Audio Recording

If you get permission to record the meeting, an AI chatbot can be prompted to create a summary from the recording. If you're unsure how to do this, just ask the AI.

> If I want you to transcribe an audio recording of a meeting into text, what steps do I take to help you do this? Give additional tips that will help you summarize a transcript accurately.

Summarize a Transcript

After the audio recording is transcribed to text, try one of these prompts.

> Use this transcript to generate a summary of the key points discussed during this meeting. The summary should include the meeting's agenda, decisions made, and any action items assigned. [insert text from recording].

> Use this transcript to summarize the monthly school board meeting. Generate a summary of the key points discussed. The summary should include the board's decisions, financial reports, and any upcoming projects. [insert text from recording].

! — A CAUTION

While AI can assist in generating the initial report, it is best to review it carefully to ensure accuracy, clarity, and alignment with the school's objectives and communication style.

47. Create Reports

? — THE PROBLEM

Roadblocks in Reporting

School leaders can struggle to find time to create detailed reports. The charge is to summarize information in a manner both comprehensive and actionable, but putting together these reports on academic performance, attendance, and other subjects is no walk in the park. This is because it is more than just pointing out what's wrong; it is about figuring out how to make things right. This process requires a good chunk of know-how, and time.

✓ — THE SOLUTION

A Revolutionary Road to Reports

Wave goodbye to another time-consuming task. AI can generate a report that includes strategies and actions for a specific goal. The tool provides language suggestions and offers improvements for report details. It can also involve analyzing data, using proven strategies, suggesting actions, and planning next steps. With the chatbot's help, you have more time to actually work on what you write in the reports.

 AN EXAMPLE

In this prompt, the AI chatbot acts as a campus team leader who wants to generate suggestions for a Targeted Improvement Plan.

 You are a school leader working on a campus with a diverse student population. Using the data provided below, generate suggestions for a Targeted Improvement Plan. The plan is a collaborative project designed by a leadership team. The actions need to result in increased student engagement and achievement. Using this baseline data, provide suggestions for goals and objectives for the plan. [Insert BASELINE DATA]

Number of students:

Grade levels on campus:

Student absentee data for each grade level:

Percentages for Diversity:

Percentages for Mobility,

Percentages for Eco-disadvantage,

Percentages for English Language Learners:

Faculty years of employment:

Continue the conversation with the following prompt, which includes academic data for the campus.

 Revise the Targeted Improvement Plan using the following ACADEMIC BASELINE: [insert data]

Math academic data for [insert] grade level:

English Language Arts academic data for [insert] grade level:

Continue the conversation with the following prompt, which includes perceptions of the campus culture.

Revise the Targeted Improvement Plan using the following BASELINE data for CAMPUS CULTURE: [insert data]

Faculty engagement survey percentages:

Family engagement survey percentages:

Student engagement survey percentages:

These examples align with ISTE Standard 3.2.d, Communicate with Stakeholders, which states, "Communicate effectively with stakeholders to gather input on the plan, celebrate successes and engage in a continuous improvement cycle."

 ACCELERATION

Revise the first draft of your report by prompting an AI platform to provide suggestions. Using the same stream, keep the conversation going until you get what you want it to say.

 Suggest ways to improve this report: [insert first draft of the report].

 Elaborate this paragraph in the report with additional information: [insert details].

 Suggest ways to insert our school's mission statement and values into this report: [insert mission and value statements].

 A CAUTION

AI can help with first drafts, but experts should review and refine the final copy. This ensures the actions align with the school's policies, resources, and the unique needs of the students and staff. While it is designed to provide accurate and helpful information, it is a machine, and the large learning model might give inaccurate responses.

Discussion Questions: Data Management and School Improvement

This chapter focused on the dynamic role of AI in data management and school improvement. Use the reflective questions below to discuss what you and your team think about AI in this role. Having these conversations can deepen understanding about how AI can simplify complicated information. The discussion can explore innovative ways to integrate AI into your school's processes and strategies.

1. How could you use AI tools with data to monitor and improve school performance? What specific insights or recommendations could AI provide? Any concerns?

2. How could AI tools assist you in generating survey questions and analyzing survey data? What advantages or efficiencies do AI tools provide in this process?

3. How could you use AI to leverage student feedback for motivation and improvement? What strategies or actions could be implemented?

4. Have you designed procedures (such as cafeteria monitoring or restroom etiquette) with the help of AI? How could AI contribute to ensuring safety, efficiency, and quality in operations?

5. Have you used AI to create summarized reports? How could AI assist in organizing and presenting complex information in a concise and meaningful manner?

Chapter 7

FAMILY AND COMMUNITY ENGAGEMENT

FOSTERING STRONG FAMILY AND COMMUNITY engagement, a paramount priority for school leaders, is the focus of chapter 7. The ideas presented in this chapter align with three ISTE Standards for leaders. The prompts contribute to strategies for communication, collaboration, and partnerships.

Discover effective communication strategies like talking points, forms, social media/web content, videos, and press releases to engage stakeholders. Celebrate success and invite participation in campus programs through organized events. Strengthen partnerships by recognizing volunteers, publishing guidebooks, soliciting donations, and communicating logistics. Leveraging community relationships also becomes crucial in responding to disasters.

This chapter will help you prioritize open communication, stakeholder involvement, and strategic partnerships to drive continuous improvement and foster a supportive, engaged school community.

Connection to the ISTE Standards for Leaders

3.2 Visionary Planner
Leaders engage others in establishing a vision, strategic plan and ongoing evaluation cycle for transforming learning with technology.

> **3.2.d** Communicate effectively with stakeholders to gather input on the plan, celebrate successes and engage in a continuous improvement cycle.

3.3 Empowering Leader
Leaders create a culture where teachers and learners are empowered to use technology in innovative ways to enrich teaching and learning.

> **3.3.c** Inspire a culture of innovation and collaboration that allows the time and space to explore and experiment with digital tools. and adoption.

3.4 Systems Designer
Leaders build teams and systems to implement, sustain and continually improve the use of technology to support learning.

> **3.4.d** Establish partnerships that support the strategic vision, achieve learning priorities and improve operations.

48. Communicate with Families and Students

THE PROBLEM

Communication Crunch

As a campus leader, you want to ensure parents are in the know about the great things happening at your school. However, social media, rumors, and news reports can sometimes get things all twisted up. You are already juggling a lot, and finding the time to keep everyone updated and informed can be a painstaking puzzle. Finding ways to keep the information flowing without piling on extra stress is hard.

THE SOLUTION

Connective Clarity

When you share the achievements of your students and teachers, you're not bragging. Your goal is to create a supportive community where everyone is informed and united. An AI aide can make it easier to reach this goal. It can help you stay in touch, keep families in the loop, and boost the overall sense of belonging and engagement. Using technology to share updates and heartwarming stories with everyone is crucial. This helps foster unity and pride. By working together and sharing information openly, you create an environment where everyone feels like they matter.

 AN EXAMPLE

In this example, I converse with an AI assistant to help keep families informed. While it takes a minute to set up the context of what I want it to say, this stream leads to a time-saving solution. In the prompt, I asked the AI to interview me by asking questions one at a time. I write answers based on details of my specific campus, and I also ask for examples or sample answers to get ideas of what to include.

 In a minute, I will ask you to write a few documents for our school. This will include blog content, Instagram posts, and an email to parents and community members. Before we begin, I want you to fully understand my school campus and the students and families who are our clients. Ask me at least 10 questions about my school campus, clients, audience, and anything else you need to complete the tasks to the best of your ability. Ask the questions one at a time, confirming you have what you need for each question.

Follow-up prompt in the same stream:

 You have the answers to all your questions. Now write a sample blog post, Instagram post, and email to parents about one of the topics you included in the answers to the question.

These examples align with ISTE Standard 3.2.d, Communicate with Stakeholders, which states, "Communicate effectively with stakeholders to gather input on the plan, celebrate successes and engage in a continuous improvement cycle."

 ACCELERATION

Here are a few more prompts to instruct the AI chatbot to take on specific roles.

School Board Member

 You are a school board member. Write a newsletter article to inform families and the community about the latest news and events at the school. This newsletter should also solicit feedback from the community.

Dean of Instruction

> You are the Dean of Instruction. Compose a friendly and informative email to parents, providing them with an overview of the events planned in the upcoming month. Please use a warm, welcoming, and helpful tone. Highlight the benefits and relevance of the upcoming events, explaining how they will contribute to the child's overall learning and academic growth. Include any other important information or details for parents. Your email should be engaging and accessible, ensuring parents can easily understand the content and feel excited about their children's upcoming learning opportunities. [Insert events]

Parent-Teacher Membership Chair

> You are the membership chair of the parent organization for our campus. Write an invitation to join the organization. Include the mission to support students and faculty of the campus. Include these details about how to join: [insert details].

49. Create Talking Points for Sticky Situations

THE PROBLEM

Delicate Dialogues

Some of the hardest conversations I had during my tenure as a principal were with family members upset about something that happened at school to their child. I tried to keep their perspective in mind—and to see them as their child's best advocate. I also strove to remain a partner in finding a solution rather than getting defensive and short. But that's a delicate dance. What is the best way to approach a difficult conversation or respond to an angry email from a parent? These sticky situations require finesse, a good deal of empathy, and the right choice of words. You may be responding to an issue the parent brings up. Or you may be addressing a difficult or sensitive topic, such as telling the parent their child is failing or bullying others. The parent may be upset and emotional, making it challenging to have a productive conversation. They may blame you for the problem, which can make it difficult to stay calm and objective. And if the conversation gets heated, it can lead to misunderstandings and further conflict. Managing those tricky exchanges mirrors teetering along a tense tightrope, painstakingly praying you can toe the fine line between truth-telling and tact.

THE SOLUTION

Empathetic Engagement

Approaches vary, but it is important to be empathetic and address concerns without adding fuel to the fire. An AI tool can help by providing you with talking points and a sample script to review before a meeting. It can also draft suggestions for how to respond in an email or letter. The AI tool can highlight key points about the problem. It can give useful tips for handling tough conversations and offer steps to solve the problem. This can all help you prepare for the conversation and express yourself clearly.

AN EXAMPLE

Here is an example of how your AI assistant can help design talking points and suggestions for a critical conversation or email.

> Your task is to respond to an angry parent in a polite and respectful tone. Design a set of talking points and a script to prepare for a) a phone call, b) a conversation in person, and c) an email. The concerns from the parent are reflected in the following email [insert email without identifying information]. Reassure them you are doing your best to solve the issue they describe. Express gratitude for the parent's feedback and patience. And highlight any actions you are taking or steps you are considering to resolve the situation.

These examples align with ISTE Standard 3.2.d, Communicate with Stakeholders, which states, "Communicate effectively with stakeholders to gather input on the plan, celebrate successes and engage in a continuous improvement cycle."

50. Write Fantastic Forms

THE PROBLEM

Time Keeps on Slippin' Slippin' Slippin'

Getting consent from parents for students to join events or support groups takes time but is necessary. To communicate effectively, you need to customize messages, address concerns, and get permissions on time. This can create a significant administrative burden for school leaders, especially counselors and academic leads, potentially hindering student access to valuable support.

 **THE SOLUTION**

Slash the Piles of Paperwork

Make it easier to get parental consent for small group intervention sessions by using AI to generate a customized letter for the program. AI can create a compelling invitation. The AI chatbot can also assist in creating a form for parents to sign, granting permission within a specified deadline. AI can help you save time on logistics so you can focus on making a positive impact on students' growth and success.

 AN EXAMPLE

Try out these steps for creating customized letters, emails, and permission forms. Use the example as a guide; tailor the content to your needs and review the suggestions.

 You are a school counselor. Write a letter in two formats: 1) to be printed on A4 paper and 2) to insert in an email. The message is addressed to families requesting permission to invite their child to a small group session. Use the following information in the letter:

Name of project:

When they will meet:

How long they will meet:

Where they will meet:

Purpose of the group:

 Next, create a permission form to print on a separate piece of A4 paper. Include a place for a signature and date to return the form.

These examples align with ISTE Standard 3.4.a, Establish Infrastructure & Systems, which states, "Lead teams to collaboratively establish the robust infrastructure and systems needed to implement the strategic plan."

51. Brainstorm Ideas for Recognizing Volunteers

 THE PROBLEM

Unseen and Underappreciated

Volunteers are the lifeblood of a thriving school, but without proper acknowledgment, they may feel undervalued, and their efforts may go unnoticed. This can harm the school atmosphere and discourage volunteers from getting involved.

 THE SOLUTION

Recognizing the Unsung Heroes

AI can help you generate many ideas to honor and appreciate the valuable contributions of volunteers. Discover creative and meaningful ways to acknowledge their invaluable efforts. AI can assist with personalized thank you notes, certificates, special events, and programs to appreciate volunteers. It gives suggestions specific to your school when you provide the details. By publicly acknowledging the hard work of volunteers, you not only show gratitude but also motivate others to join and strengthen your school community.

 AN EXAMPLE

This example enlists the AI thought partner in a brainstorming session to establish a system for recognizing and sustaining a program that appreciates school volunteers.

 Brainstorm new ideas for recognizing volunteers on a school campus. Provide ideas such as [insert preferences, e.g., personalized thank you notes, certificates of appreciation, organizing special events, or implementing volunteer appreciation programs]. Express gratitude and highlight volunteers' efforts to foster a positive and inclusive school culture. Encourage continued involvement.

This example aligns with ISTE Standard 3.4.a, Establish Infrastructure & Systems, which states, "Lead teams to collaboratively establish the robust infrastructure and systems needed to implement the strategic plan."

52. Publish a Guidebook for Volunteers

 THE PROBLEM

Navigating the Guidebook Maze

Putting together a useful guidebook can be a complex undertaking. The process can feel as if you are finding your way through an intricate maze. You want to create a resource customized for your program's specific objectives and culture. It should communicate key details in a clear, comprehensible manner. And, of course, you need to cover the fundamentals—outline goals, detail job duties, and establish protocol. But a top-notch guide requires thoughtful fine-tuning on deeper levels as well. All this takes a good amount of time and steadfast attention if you hope to get it right.

 THE SOLUTION

Guiding the Way

AI has the potential to improve the process of creating guidebooks in less time with greater detail. It can automate tasks such as gathering and organizing information, generating text, translating languages, and providing feedback. This can save time and effort for writers. An AI assistant can ensure the guidebook is well-written, informative, and accessible to a wider audience.

 AN EXAMPLE

Create an outline with this prompt for a guidebook to use in a school's volunteer program.

> Suggest an outline of topics to use in a guidebook for volunteers at our school campus.

After you have decided on the topics you want to include in the guidebook, write each section with suggestions from AI.

> Next, create a comprehensive and user-friendly resource for volunteers by including details for each topic [insert topic list]. Include a famous quote about gratitude for their service in the conclusion.

This example aligns with ISTE Standard 3.4.a, Establish Infrastructure & Systems, which states, "Lead teams to collaboratively establish the robust infrastructure and systems needed to implement the strategic plan."

53. Elicit Suggestions for a Presentation

 THE PROBLEM

Presentation Blues

When presenting information at family night, our team would always work to create an engaging and impactful experience. But that can be a daunting and time-consuming task. Often we would struggle to come up with fresh ideas. This challenge can result in a lackluster presentation that fails to convey the information effectively or engage the listeners.

 THE SOLUTION

A Just Right Jazzy Prez

An AI assistant can help jazz up your next presentation. Let it spark ideas for an interesting introduction. Ask it for ideas to complete an outline, add content, and describe images for the slides. You can get it to improve the tone, add humor or personal stories, and make the introduction match your audience. Why brainstorm alone when the AI assistant can help make your presentation better?

 AN EXAMPLE

In this prompt, the AI assists in preparing a presentation for families by a team of six teachers.

 You are part of a team of six teachers on the middle school campus. The team is preparing a presentation for families at the Meet the Teacher event. Write an outline and delegate topics to each member of the team. Provide talking points for each section of the presentation. Provide suggestions for the presentation visuals.

These examples align with ISTE Standard 3.2.d, Build a Strategic Plan, which states, "Communicate effectively with stakeholders to gather input on the plan, celebrate successes and engage in a continuous improvement cycle."

 **ACCELERATION**

If you want to add jokes to your presentation, give it a try. You can decide if the joke landed, and if it fell flat, tell the AI comedian to try again.

 Tell a joke about the scarcity of time for a busy family with kids.

54. Discover Your Inner Artist

 **THE PROBLEM**

Visual Vexations

Have you ever struggled to find the perfect image for a school flier or presentation? I know the struggle all too well. Trying to find the perfect and free image would take forever. Traditionally, this might mean hiring a graphic designer, hunting for (and paying for) stock photos, or settling for limited clip art options—all time-consuming, expensive, or restrictive.

 THE SOLUTION

Image Innovation

With AI, you can easily create custom visuals that perfectly capture your message. This can save you time and ensure your audience sits up and takes notice. It's like magic: just describe what you need, and AI whips up a unique image. Canva, along with many other generative AI image creation tools, offers a wide range of artistic styles you can use in your prompts.

 AN EXAMPLE

The following prompt was used with Canva. Note that it describes a topic and a style of art.

 Generate a warm and inviting watercolor illustration of a diverse group of students showcasing their school projects at an open house. Parents observe with smiles, and teachers answer questions.

These examples align with ISTE Standard 3.3.c, Inspire a Culture of Innovation, which states, "Inspire a culture of innovation and collaboration that allows the time and space to explore and experiment with digital tools and adoption."

FIGURE 7.1 Image AI-generated by Canva.

55. Create Social Media and Webpage Content

 THE PROBLEM

Media Madness

Connecting with your school community using social media and a professional web page can increase engagement. However, if the posts and content are not carefully crafted, an online presence can appear unprofessional and fail to connect with the intended audience. When this happens, you miss out on sharing interesting news, advertising important events, and building an online community. And without the assistance of AI tools, managing and optimizing this process can be incredibly time-consuming.

 THE SOLUTION

Super Social Sightings

AI tools can streamline the process of creating impactful social media posts, enabling efficient communication of crucial information, fostering audience relationships, and enhancing community engagement. These tools significantly simplify the task by saving time and incorporating elements like hashtags and emojis.

AN EXAMPLE

When creating a prompt to publicize a school event, clearly define the target audience for the social media post. Provide specific details about the event being promoted and include how many posts you want generated.

> Write [insert number, e.g., 10] posts for social media, targeting [insert audience, e.g., families of students]. Each post will advertise the event, [insert name of event, e.g., "End of Year Awards Ceremony"] for [insert name of school]. Include date [insert], time [insert], location [insert], emojis, and hashtags.

These examples align with ISTE Standard 3.3.c, Inspire a Culture of Innovation, which states, "Inspire a culture of innovation and collaboration that allows the time and space to explore and experiment with digital tools and adoption."

ACCELERATION

Learn How to Use Social Media

Not only does AI assist with content creation, but it can also help you learn how to improve your social media skills.

> How can I leverage social media to engage parents in school activities? What precautions should I take when using social media that involves school children?

Focus on a Specific Topic

AI can assist in writing social media posts for a variety of topics.

> Write 10 messages ready to share on social media channels. Focus on [insert topic, e.g., bullying, reading at home, after-school pickup procedures]. The intended audience is [insert audience, e.g., students, parents, staff, broader school community]. Include captions and hashtags as needed.

Include an Image Generated by AI

Use AI systems to create custom visuals from text prompts, allowing leaders to produce images for social media content that perfectly captures their message.

> Generate a unique social media graphic to promote an upcoming event [e.g., science fairs, book fairs, or athletic events]. The image is intended to grab attention and boost participation.

Create a Schedule

Create a schedule for posting social media messages. The AI can format the schedule in a table and prepare posts to launch on a timeline. When you're consistent and strategic with your posting schedule, you create more effective messages and save precious time.

> Create a table that defines the frequency of posting social media messages. Schedule [insert number, e.g., 5] posts only on Monday through Friday. Designate messages to target a specific audience type: [insert audience, e.g., parents, students, or community leaders]. Suggest topics using these ideas [insert events, e.g., start of school, open house].

Design Your Professional Webpage

Need ideas for the school webpage about yourself?

> Create suggestions for a personal webpage to use on the campus website. Use the following information. Then, ask me questions about any other content regarding an effective website:
>
> 1. Purpose and Content:
>
> The primary purpose of my webpage is [insert details].
>
> Focus on my work with [insert name of school].
>
> Specific content to include [insert details, e.g., biography, blog, resources for educators, travel experiences].
>
> 2. Design Preferences:
>
> Give suggestions for specific design preferences [insert details, e.g., colors, themes, or styles; more professional or creative tone, or a mix of both].
>
> 3. Contact and Social Media:
>
> Include any contact information or links to social media profiles [insert details and links you are comfortable sharing on a public platform].

56. Launch a Video Presentation

 THE PROBLEM

Lost in Translation

Video is a great way to communicate with families, especially since phones are so ubiquitous. But videos are time-consuming to create, and without a clear message, families may miss important information. This can lead to confusion, missed appointments, and a lack of active participation from parents, affecting the success of events and the collaboration between parents and teachers.

 THE SOLUTION

Script Success

Regardless of your experience in video scriptwriting, AI can help you craft a clear, concise, and engaging script. This tool gives advice on organizing the script, including important details, and using engaging language to inform parents and the community.

 AN EXAMPLE

When using this prompt, notice how it clearly defines the video's target audience. You will need to provide specific details about the content presentation's content, such as the purpose, topic, or event being discussed. Also include the desired length of the video in minutes and any additional instructions or requirements.

 Write a 1-minute script to read aloud for a video clip to send to families of [insert name of school]. Describe the expectations for an upcoming parent-teacher conference day. Use compelling language to engage and inform busy families.

Purpose / Topic: [insert details].

Include these reminders: 1) Bring questions, 2) arrive on time, 3) include your child.

Include date [insert] and location [insert].

Include additional information: [insert details, e.g., each student's specific conference time will be sent in an email from the classroom teacher.

These examples align with ISTE Standard 3.3.c, Inspire a Culture of Innovation, which states, "Inspire a culture of innovation and collaboration that allows the time and space to explore and experiment with digital tools and adoption."

ACCELERATION

AI helps write a good video script and suggests graphics and visuals to improve it. By including graphics, such as infographics, charts, or images, you can increase the visual appeal and value of the video. AI can suggest the best graphics for data, key points, and concepts.

When you're ready to add the images, try out generative AI tools such as DALL•E or Midjourney. These platforms can be used to create images from a text prompt. They offer a great way to create custom images not available elsewhere. Several platforms also can process images along with your prompt.

> Suggest images to use in a 30-second public service announcement video about school lunches. Include date [insert], time [insert], and location [insert]. Also include the following information: [insert details]. Capture the attention of the audience with engaging ideas.

57. Invite Participation in a Mentoring Program

THE PROBLEM

Pleading for Participation

Struggling students can thrive with the support of volunteer tutors. Yet, recruiting these volunteers can be a hurdle. While mentoring and tutoring programs offer a wealth of benefits to students, effectively communicating the need for volunteers and igniting their passion to participate is crucial. Uninspiring or unclear calls to action risk going unnoticed, hindering program growth and its ability to reach students who need it most.

THE SOLUTION

Persuasion Pave the Way

AI can help you create an informative and attention-grabbing invitation. The tool can give tips on how to write the content, showcase the perks of volunteering, or revise success stories shared with you. It can also ensure inclusivity and alignment with the school's goals.

AN EXAMPLE

When creating the prompt, clearly define the target audience for the invitation. Provide specific details about the content of the email, including the purpose, benefits, and significance of the program. Include instructions on how to convey the message effectively and motivate potential volunteers to get involved. Then, customize and refine the selected suggestions to fit your specific context.

> Generate an invitation to community members to participate in a mentoring and tutoring program. The invitation must include clear instructions on how individuals can get involved in the program or ask questions. Incorporate our school's values, reflect inclusivity, and consider the diverse backgrounds of potential volunteers. Clearly communicate the benefits and the process. Include the following information and anything else you know to be effective for recruiting volunteers:
>
> Audience: parents and community members
>
> Purpose of the project: [insert]
>
> School's values: [insert]
>
> Date: [insert] Times: [insert] Location: [insert school address]
>
> Requirements (e.g., completing a volunteer background process for the school district): [insert details, e.g., fill out a form online].
>
> How to ask questions or learn more about the program.

These examples align with ISTE Standard 3.2.d, Communicate with Stakeholders, which states, "Communicate effectively with stakeholders to gather input on the plan, celebrate successes and engage in a continuous improvement cycle."

ACCELERATION

Using the same stream, prompt the AI tool to generate suggestions for the invitation format, such as a form on paper or a website. Request guidance on how to use personal anecdotes, success stories, or testimonials to create an emotional connection with potential volunteers.

> Describe the volunteer program for an A4 page of paper, webpage, and social media post.

> Provide suggestions on how to use a story of a mentor who shares his experience working with students in the mentoring program.

Translate this description of the mentoring program into another language [insert language].

58. Respond to Disaster

 THE PROBLEM

Communicating Crises

As a school district's Communication Director, I witnessed firsthand the urgency of clear and timely communication during a crisis or disaster response. Despite creating templates beforehand, the dynamic nature of a crisis demanded a fast and nimble approach.

Disaster communication materials ideally cover evacuation plans, first aid procedures, and survival tips. To ensure inclusivity, they must be culturally sensitive and readily understood across all literacy levels. This might necessitate translation into multiple languages or the use of clear visuals. The dynamic nature of disasters demands adaptability and flexibility in these materials.

 THE SOLUTION

Template Triumphs

I would have loved to have a personal assistant for crisis and disaster planning. AI can create customizable templates for different emergencies. These pre-built templates could include evacuation plans, emergency contacts, shelter information, and even first-aid instructions. They would act as a foundation for vital materials like public service announcements and brochures. During a crisis, these AI templates, combined with trusted sources, would dramatically speed up the creation of critical resources. This translates to faster information sharing with affected communities, empowering them to make informed decisions and prioritize safety.

 AN EXAMPLE

When creating this type of prompt, specify the type of disaster for which the response materials are needed, such as earthquake, hurricane, pandemic, or security threat. Include the key information, such as emergency contacts, evacuation procedures, shelter locations, first aid instructions, safety protocols, or available resources. Modify content to reflect local protocols, available resources, and community specifics.

> Create a public service announcement (PSA) from the school about the recent natural disaster. Address the message to parents and families of the school community. Explain the school response [insert details]. Describe services available in the community. Use plain language. Avoid acronyms. Include this information:
>
> Name of school: [insert name].
>
> When the school will be closed for repairs: [dates]
>
> What community resources are available to assist: [Insert details].
>
> For more information: [insert phone, website].

These examples align with ISTE Standard 3.2.d, Communicate with Stakeholders, which states, "Communicate effectively with stakeholders to gather input on the plan, celebrate successes and engage in a continuous improvement cycle."

A CAUTION

Make sure to go over the disaster response materials with district personnel who specialize in this area. An expert reviewer as a second set of eyes is a priority. By working with district experts in disasters, the templates can improve and continue to keep the school community informed in difficult situations.

59. Create a Press Release for the Media

THE PROBLEM

Fumbling the News

Schools can struggle to effectively share new developments or initiatives with the media and public. A good press release shares accurate information in a timely manner, and expert skills are needed to communicate to the public effectively.

THE SOLUTION

PR Perfection

In this example, the AI tool illustrates how it can help write a press release faster and easier than you can write it on your own. It can help you hit the mark with powerful suggestions. If you need ideas on highlighting key points and using captivating language, try using an AI to help you get started.

AN EXAMPLE

This example demonstrates how an AI chatbot can generate press releases to announce a new hire. Start by sharing the main topic of your announcement, be it a new hire, an event, an academic milestone, or the start of a new program. Provide crucial details pertinent to the announcement, such as names, dates, or descriptions. Consider including actual quotes from school officials or other stakeholders. Lastly, make sure you supply the contact information of the school's representative for any further media inquiries.

> Write a press release to announce a new hire for the school campus. Include the following information:
>
> Name of newly hired employee: use "name"
>
> Name of person they are replacing: use "name"
>
> Previous employment: [insert info]
>
> Years of experience in education: [insert info]
>
> Announce meet and greet [date], [time] and [location].
>
> Contact information of the school's PR representative: use "name", "phone," "email"
>
> About our school: [insert a brief background or history of the school, highlighting any notable achievements, programs, or unique features].
>
> Quote from the principal: [insert quote].

This example aligns with ISTE Standard 3.2.d, Communicate with Stakeholders, which states, "Communicate effectively with stakeholders to gather input on the plan, celebrate successes and engage in a continuous improvement cycle."

A CAUTION

The use of AI-generated language resulted in unintended consequences when used for a press release at Vanderbilt University. The administrator sent an email to students generated by an AI language model regarding COVID-19 protocols. The email caused concern and led to a public apology and resignation (Levine, 2023). AI can generate the initial draft of a press release, but the content should always be reviewed and edited by a human with expertise in public relations or communications. This is important to ensure accuracy, clarity, and adherence to any organizational guidelines or policies. Human review is necessary to ensure it represents the school's voice and maintains a professional standard.

60. Solicit Donations

 THE PROBLEM

Financial Frustrations

Whoever said money can't buy happiness clearly never tried to fund a school project. Schools often have to find money for various projects or events, but securing financial support can be a daunting task. It is difficult to find the time to write a persuasive letter, and motivating donors means coming up with creative ideas. A standard appeal letter is not enough to get potential donors' attention and support in today's competitive fundraising world.

 THE SOLUTION

AI-Powered Persuasion

Improve fundraising projects by using AI to get attention. Create personalized letters that connect with donors in a unique way. The letters can match the donors' interests and motivations with the school's needs. This level of personalization goes beyond simply addressing the donor by name. Let the AI craft a creative narrative to illustrate the real effects of your school's projects.

 AN EXAMPLE

In this prompt, the AI assistant will use key information to generate an email to solicit donations and help you get moving on your next project or idea. If you also mail a letter to the businesses, create a mail merge. Not sure how to merge mail? Ask your assistant.

> Generate a donation solicitation letter and email for a school initiative. Ensure the letter is compelling and transparent in its appeal to potential contributors. Include the following information:
>
> Purpose of the donations: [Insert purpose, e.g., staff appreciation]
>
> Name of school campus: [Insert name]
>
> School address: [insert address]
>
> How to donate: include delivery, pick up, or online [website link],
>
> Contact information: "name", "phone", "email".
>
> Suggested donations: gift cards, products, services
>
> How funding matches the donor's mission: [insert details about the potential donor].

This example aligns with ISTE Standard 3.4.d, Establish Strategic Partnerships, which states, "Establish partnerships that support the strategic vision, achieve learning priorities and improve operations."

61. Outline and Organize an Event

 ●──── **THE PROBLEM**

Career Day Conundrum

Career days help students learn about different careers, get advice from professionals, and make future choices. However, to have a successful career day, you need to plan and organize it carefully. This can take an exorbitant amount of time and effort. I was lucky to work with a fantastic Assistant Principal who organized an amazing Career Day for our school. But I wonder how AI would have worked in the mix?

 ●──── **THE SOLUTION**

A Captivating Career Day

AI can help create a well-organized and engaging career day by guiding the structure and content of the event. You can use it to plan the event, choose activities, and make sure the content is helpful for students. Use the AI tool also to get more information and ideas about specific steps for planning and executing the big day.

 ●──── **AN EXAMPLE**

Use this prompt to help your team create a captivating career day. Find ways to inspire students and support academic goals.

This example aligns with ISTE Standard 3.4.d, Establish Strategic Partnerships, which states, "Establish partnerships that support the strategic vision, achieve learning priorities and improve operations."

> Design a successful career day for high school students.
>
> Write specific goals and objectives of the career day event, such as exposing students to different career options, facilitating networking opportunities, or providing hands-on experiences.
>
> Brainstorm the types of professionals to invite, considering a diverse range of careers, industries, and expertise. Suggest types of engaging speakers who can inspire and educate students about their respective fields.
>
> Create an agenda that includes keynote speeches, panel discussions, workshops, interactive activities, or career fair-style booths.
>
> Recommend sufficient time for each session to ensure a well-paced and engaging event. Then, advise on logistical considerations, such as venue selection, equipment needs, volunteer coordination, and resource allocation.
>
> Provide tips on maximizing available resources, leveraging technology, and ensuring a smooth and successful event execution.

62. Communicate Logistics for Student Trips

THE PROBLEM

Cryptic Communication

While my childhood school days hold many memories, some of the most cherished experiences were the field trips. Transporting students into the community on educational field trips is important, but organizing these trips requires clear communication and well-defined logistics. Gathering and documenting logistical information like dates, costs, and permission slips is necessary but time-consuming. Sharing this information with different departments like administration and transportation, as well as families, needs to be efficient or it will lead to errors, delays, and miscommunication. A clear system of operation is needed to streamline communication and manage logistics for student field trips, ensuring a safe, smooth, and efficient planning process for all stakeholders.

THE SOLUTION

Logistics Wizardry

Here's where a touch of magic can come in. AI can become your partner in this operation, streamlining communication to school departments and families. Imagine this helpful tool whipping up permission slips and collecting information with ease, freeing you up to focus on the educational adventure itself.

AN EXAMPLE

Try out the prompt below to create a template. Some AI platforms, like Google's Gemini, will create spreadsheets to hold information about the field trip. The information can drop into columns and rows, ready for you to export.

Create a spreadsheet to provide the logistics of a field trip for students. Use 3 columns with these headers: Topic, Details, Sample Information

Include the following information as rows:

TRIP DETAILS: Date of the trip; Departure and return times; Destination name and address; Purpose or objectives of the trip

CLASS/GRADE INFORMATION: Grade level or class going on the trip; Number of students participating; Number of teachers and chaperones accompanying the students

EMERGENCY CONTACTS: Contact information for the school administrator or coordinator in case of emergencies; Contact information for a faculty member in charge during the trip

TRANSPORTATION: Mode of transportation (bus, vans, etc.); Departure location; Return location

MEDICAL INFORMATION: Any specific medical conditions or allergies of participating students; Details about any necessary medications and instructions

PERMISSIONS: Parental consent for the student to participate in the field trip; Authorization for emergency medical treatment; Photo release consent for taking pictures during the trip

SPECIAL ACCOMMODATIONS: Any special accommodations needed for students with disabilities or specific requirements

ITINERARY: List of activities and locations planned for the trip, including estimated times

LUNCH AND SNACKS: Information on whether lunch will be provided or if students need to bring their own; Details about snacks or meals during the trip

CHAPERONE INFORMATION: List of chaperones and their contact information; Responsibilities assigned to each chaperone

COST AND PAYMENT: Total cost per student; Payment instructions and deadlines

ADDITIONAL NOTES: Any additional instructions or information for parents, students, or chaperones

APPROVAL AND SIGNATURE: Space for a school administrator's approval or signature; Space for a faculty member's signature

This example aligns with ISTE Standard 3.4.d, Establish Strategic Partnerships, which states, "Establish partnerships that support the strategic vision, achieve learning priorities and improve operations."

 ACCELERATION

In the next two examples, the prompt continues the conversation about the school field trip described above. Be sure to use this prompt in the same stream as the previous prompt for the best results.

 Create two emails communicating information about the field trip. Write one email to the transportation department and the second email to the school's cafeteria. Use the information from the previous prompt in the email. Describe the specific logistical information, including transportation arrangements and pick-up and drop-off times and locations.

 Write an email for a student field trip to the families of students going on the field trip. The purpose of the trip is to [insert details about academic benefits]. Use the information from the previous prompt in the email. Describe the specific logistical details, including transportation arrangements, pick-up and drop-off times and locations, and special instructions or requirements. Include any other relevant details for a comprehensive and accurate message.

 A CAUTION

When using AI with emails, always review the content to ensure accuracy, clarity, and alignment with the school's policies and procedures—before hitting "Send."

Building Bridges:
How One Principal Used AI to Deepen Family Engagement
Andy Hagman

In March 2024, Andrew Hagman, principal of Momentous School in Dallas, Texas, embarked on a mission to strengthen family engagement with the help of AI. He chose to focus on the topic "Create Social Media and Webpage Content" in chapter 7, Family and Community Engagement. Andy explored how AI could address engagement while considering one particular need of his community: More than 80% of families attending the school qualify for free or reduced-price lunch. Social media, a powerful tool for bridging divides, seemed like a promising solution. But could it work for this situation?

AI to the Rescue. Andrew turned to Google Gemini with a sample prompt from this book and then revised it to focus more closely on his school's situation, asking, "How can I leverage social media to engage lower-income parents in school activities?" This shift from a broad question to a targeted one unlocked the AI's potential, and the AI responded with a comprehensive action plan.

AI's Tailored Response. Understanding data limitations, AI emphasized creating short, text-based posts. It also championed storytelling, suggesting posts that highlight the benefits of parent involvement and showcase past successes. Recognizing the school's diverse community, AI recommended translating key messages to be inclusive.

Engagement Strategies. Other ideas included interactive features like polls and Q&A sessions to address common concerns. AI also suggested fostering a closed Facebook group for parents to connect and support each other.

AI vs. a Traditional Online Search. Reflecting on the experience, Andrew contrasted AI's suggestions to the responses from a traditional search: "The non-AI search produced 15,500,000 responses. In the first two or three pages of results, sometimes all aspects of the prompt were addressed, but there was usually something missing, such as an emphasis on lower-income parents."

A Model for Others. Andrew's story, with concrete strategies and personal experience, serves as an example for school leaders. He says, "The potential is tremendous because you get a meta-analysis with suggestions, all in one location, rather than having to comb through multiple sites and synthesize the information." His experience demonstrates how AI can be an invaluable tool to address campus-specific needs—such as building stronger family connections—ultimately creating a more inclusive and supportive school community.

Andy Hagman has more than 27 years of experience in public education, including nine years as a high school principal, five years as a junior high principal, five years as an assistant principal, and eight years as a mathematics teacher.

Discussion Questions: Family and Community Engagement

AI can offer new ways to interact with families and the community. Ideas offered in this chapter can lead to more inclusive and strong relationships with all who support your school. Discuss these questions with your team to see how AI can help enrich partnerships and build community engagement.

1. In what ways could you engage parents and the wider community with the help of AI? If you've tried it, were you satisfied with the outcome of your efforts?

2. In what ways could you recognize and appreciate volunteers with AI's help? How could AI contribute to the culture of gratitude and support within the school community?

3. In what ways could you use AI to engage parents and the community with social media content? How could AI contribute to expanding reach, increasing engagement, and fostering meaningful interactions?

4. What are you finding is the most effective way to communicate important information during noteworthy events or disasters? How could AI contribute to ensuring timely and relevant communication, keeping the community informed and fostering a sense of security?

5. When organizing career days or coordinating logistics for student trips, what elements are important to include? How could AI contribute to the planning and execution process?

A LAST WORD

This book has explored how artificial intelligence can be a powerful ally on the road to productivity and work-life balance. It aims to reveal a new way for educators to navigate the intricate landscape of modern schools. The examples provided are merely the seeds from which a healthier and more efficient educational environment can grow.

As AI continues to evolve, doubling its capabilities approximately every six months (Sevilla et al., 2022), the possibilities it presents are not just transformative but essential. It's time for the education system to embrace this change. Then, I believe, educators will be better equipped to focus on what truly matters: taking better care of themselves while inspiring the minds of the next generation.

Let this book be a guide, a starting point, for school leaders to harness the power of AI in creating a dynamic and joyful learning community. The future of education, empowered by artificial intelligence, is not just a dream. It is a tangible, achievable reality, and the journey begins now.

An Algorithm as an Impressionist Painting, created with DALL·E by OpenAI.

APPENDIX

AI Resources

In this appendix, you'll discover a variety of helpful tools and resources. Many of them are available at no cost. Please note that the technology landscape is rapidly changing, so these tools may be updated or replaced over time. For the most current information on new tools or changes, visit my website at vickieechols.com. Best wishes for a fulfilling and creative journey.

Bringing AI to School: Tips for School Leaders
ISTE (2023)
tinyurl.com/Bringing-AI-to-School

Hands On AI Projects: A Guide on Ethics and AI
ISTE (2023)
tinyurl.com/Hands-On-AI-Projects

AI Guidance For Schools Toolkit
Code.org (2023)
https://www.teachai.org/toolkit

Basic Glossary

The following glossary was generated by AI and can serve as a starting point for educators to familiarize themselves with key concepts.

Top 10 Generative AI Terms for Educators:

1. **Generative AI.** Technology that creates entirely new content, such as text, images, or code, based on what it has learned from existing data.

2. **Large Language Model (LLM).** A powerful AI model trained on massive amounts of text data, allowing it to generate human-quality writing, translate languages, and answer questions.

3. **Deep Learning.** A type of machine learning that uses complex neural networks to analyze data and learn patterns, often used in generative AI.

4. **Machine Learning (ML).** A field of AI where computers learn from data without explicit programming. This allows them to improve their performance over time.

5. **Prompt.** A specific instruction or question given to a generative AI model to guide its output.

6. **Training Data.** The massive amount of data (text, images, code) that generative AI models are trained on to learn how to create new content.

7. **Bias.** Potential influence in a generative AI model's output based on the data it was trained on. Educators need to be aware of potential biases and use models critically.

8. **Natural Language Processing (NLP).** A subfield of AI that deals with the interaction between computers and human language. This is crucial for LLMs and other generative AI models that work with text.

9. **Output.** The content (text, image, code) a generative AI model produces in response to a prompt.

10. **Ethical Considerations.** The potential impact and responsible use of generative AI, including issues like bias, misinformation, and plagiarism. It's important for educators to discuss these with students.

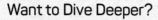

Want to Dive Deeper?

These experts offer a more comprehensive glossary of terms:

AI Glossary. Andreessen Horowitz

ChatGPT Glossary. 42 AI terms that everyone should know; CNET

AI Glossary. Artificial intelligence, in so many words; Matthew Hutson, *Science*

Artificial Intelligence Glossary. Neural networks and other terms explained; Adam Pasik, *The New York Times*

ISTE Standards Aligned with Related Topics

The ISTE Education Leader Standards provide a framework for integrating technology to promote forward-thinking educational practices.

EDUCATION LEADER STANDARD	DESCRIPTION	TOPIC NUMBER
3.1 Equity and Citizenship Advocate	Leaders use technology to increase equity, inclusion and digital citizenship practices.	Topics: 1-5, 7, 17
3.2 Visionary Planner	Leaders engage others in establishing a vision, strategic plan and ongoing evaluation cycle for transforming learning with technology.	Topics: 8, 34-39, 45-49, 53, 57-59
3.3 Empowering Leader	Leaders create a culture where teachers and learners are empowered to use technology in innovative ways to enrich teaching and learning.	Topics: 12-16, 19, 30, 54-56
3.4 Systems Designer	Leaders build teams and systems to implement, sustain and continually improve the use of technology to support learning.	Topics: 40-45, 50-52, 60-62
3.5 Connected Learner	Leaders model and promote continuous professional learning for themselves and others.	Topics: 9-11, 18, 20-29, 31-33

REFERENCES

Abdul-Jabbar, K. (2023). *What happens when Kareem attends his first AI conference.* Kareem Abdul-Jabbar Substack. https://kareem.substack.com/p/what-happens-when-kareem-attends?utm_medium=email&utm_source=multiple-personal-recommendations-email

Andreessen M. (n.d.). *AI glossary.* Andreessen Horowitz (a16z). https://a16z.com/ai-glossary/

Andreessen, M. (2023). *Why AI will save the world.* Andreessen Horowitz (a16z). https://a16z.com/2023/06/06/ai-will-save-the-world/

Baeder, J. (2017). *10 questions for better feedback on teaching.* The Principal Center. https://www.principalcenter.com/wp-content/uploads/10-questions-better-feedback.pdf

Baeder, J. (2017). *Now we're talking! 21 days to high-performance instructional leadership.* Solution Tree Press.

Bambrick-Santoyo, P., & Lemov, D. (2017). *Leverage leadership 2.0: A practical guide to building exceptional schools.* Jossey-Bass.

Buolamwini, J. (2016). *How I'm fighting bias in algorithms* [Transcript]. TED Conferences. https://www.ted.com/talks/joy_buolamwini_how_i_m_fighting_bias_in_algorithms/transcript?language=en

Caballero, C. (2023). *Developing a school master plan.* Edutopia. https://www.edutopia.org/article/developing-school-master-plan

Cardona M., Rodriquez R., Ismael K., (2023). *Artificial intelligence and the future of teaching and learning* [PDF]. U.S. Department of Education. https://www2.ed.gov/documents/ai-report/ai-report.pdf

Content Technologies Inc. (n.d.). https://contenttechnologiesinc.com/

Cooper, R., & Murphy, E. (2016). *Hacking project-based learning: 10 easy steps to PBL and inquiry in the classroom.* Times 10 Publications.

Delahooke, M. (2019). *Beyond behaviors: Using brain science and compassion to understand and solve children's behavioral challenges.* Tantor and Blackstone Publishing.

DeMatthews, D. E. (2021). *We're facing a looming crisis of principal burnout.* Education Week. https://www.edweek.org/leadership/opinion-were-facing-a-looming-crisis-of-principal-burnout/2021/10

DeWitt, P. M. (2016). *Collaborative Leadership: Six influences that matter most.* Corwin.

Fullan, M., & Matsuda, M. (2024). *Emotional intelligence and AI together can help lessen the student mental health crisis (Opinion).* Education Week. https://www.edweek.org/leadership/opinion-emotional-intelligence-and-ai-together-can-help-lessen-the-student-mental-health-crisis/2024/01

Gaskell, M. (2023) *New ways to harness feedback in leading your school to success.* SmartBrief, https://corp.smartbrief.com/original/2023/06/feedback-using-ai-chatbot

Gaskell, M. (2024). *How school leaders can address the inequities of the AI digital divide.* TechLearning. https://www.techlearning.com/news/how-school-leaders-can-address-the-inequities-of-the-ai-digital-divide

Gecker, J. (2023). *Amid ChatGPT outcry, some teachers are inviting AI to class.* AP News. https://apnews.com/article/chatgpt-ai-use-school-essay-7bc171932ff9b994e04f6eaefc09319f

Goldring, E., Grissom, J., Neumerski, C., Murphy, J., Blissett, R., & Porter, A. (2015). *Making time for instructional leadership* (vol. 1). Wallace Foundation. https://www.wallacefoundation.org/knowledge-center/Documents/Making-Time-for-Instructional-Leadership-Vol-1.pdf

Grant, A. (Host). (2023). ChatGPT did NOT title this podcast (w/ Allie Miller & Ethan Mollick) [Audio podcast episdode]. In *WorkLife with Adam Grant.* https://open.spotify.com/episode/4SDz39mhB9juGO5TgSc4NO?si=k23vko1PQqKVnXWDVCkR5A&nd=1

Gratas, B. (2023). *50 ChatGPT statistics and facts you need to know.* InvGate. https://blog.invgate.com/chatgpt-statistics

Grissom, J. A., Egalite, A. J., & Lindsay, C. A. (2013). *How principals affect students and schools: A systematic synthesis of two decades of research* [Executive summary]. The Wallace Foundation. https://www.wallacefoundation.org/knowledge-center/pages/how-principals-affect-students-and-schools-executive-summary.aspx#implications_for_policymakers

Helmore, E. (2023). *We are a little bit scared: OpenAI CEO warns of risks of artificial intelligence.* The Guardian. https://www.theguardian.com/technology/2023/mar/17/openai-sam-altman-artificial-intelligence-warning-gpt4

Horn, E. (2023). *How to create a responsible use policy for AI.* TCEA Blog. https://blog.tcea.org/responsible-use-policy-ai/

Howard, T. (2022). *Start the school year with Purpose.* Here are 5 priorities. Education Week. https://www.edweek.org/leadership/opinion-start-the-school-year-with-purpose-here-are-5-priorities/2022/08

Hutson, M. (2017). AI glossary: Artificial intelligence, in so many words. *Science, 357*(6346), 19. https://doi.org/10.1126/science.357.6346.19

Hyman, L. (2023). It's not the end of work. It's the end of boring work [Opinion]. *The New York Times.* https://www.nytimes.com/2023/04/22/opinion/jobs-ai-chatgpt.html?campaign_id=39&emc=edit_ty_20230422&instance_id=90831&nl=opinion-today&regi_id=85176147&segment_id=131102&te=1&user_id=f601b05458b8ee1a79ff63056ace9f98

International Society for Technology in Education. (2018). ISTE standards. https://iste.org/standards

International Society for Technology in Education. (2023). *Bringing AI to school: Tips for school leaders* [Guide]. https://cdn.iste.org/www-root/2023-07/Bringing_AI_to_School-2023_07.pdf

Kennedy, K. (2023). *The mind-body connection for educators: Intentional movement for wellness.* Jossey-Bass.

Kennedy, K. (2023). *"Time does not heal all wounds...": A call for healing and system-level changes.* Wellness for Educators. https://well4edu.org/blog/time-does-not-heal-all-wounds

Khan, I. (2023). *ChatGPT glossary: 42 AI terms that everyone should know.* CNET. https://www.cnet.com/tech/computing/chatgpt-glossary-42-ai-terms-that-everyone-should-know/

Khan, I. (2023). *ChatGPT vs. Bing vs. Google Bard: Which AI is the most helpful?* CNET. https://www.cnet.com/tech/services-and-software/chatgpt-vs-bing-vs-google-Bard-which-ai-is-the-most-helpful/

Koch, R. (1999). *The 80/20 principle: The secret to achieving more with less.* Crown Currency.

LaHayne, S. P. (2023). *Adolescents need more proactive, preventative mental health supports in school.* EdSurge News. https://www.edsurge.com/news/2023-03-24-adolescents-need-more-proactive-preventative-mental-health-supports-in-school

Lavigne, H., Shakman, K., Zweig, J., & Greller, S. (2016). *Principals' time, tasks, and professional development: An analysis of schools and staffing survey data* [PDF]. Education Development Center, Inc. https://files.eric.ed.gov/fulltext/ED569168.pdf

Levine, S. (2023). *Vanderbilt apologizes for using ChatGPT in email on Michigan shooting.* The Guardian. https://www.theguardian.com/us-news/2023/feb/22/vanderbilt-chatgpt-ai-michigan-shooting-email

MacIntosh, S. & Rowley, J. (2021). *How bias affects our perceptions of data: 3 ways to guard against unconscious bias.* Education Elements. https://www.edelements.com/blog/how-bias-affects-our-perception-of-data-3-ways-to-guard-against-unconscious-bias

Mahfouz, J. (2020). Principals and stress: Few coping strategies for abundant stressors. *Educational Management Administration & Leadership, 48*(3), 440–458. https://doi.org/10.1177/1741143218817562

Marcus, G., & Luccioni, S. (2023). *Stop treating AI models Like people.* Marcus on AI [Substack]. https://garymarcus.substack.com/p/stop-treating-ai-models-like-people

McClennen, N., & Poth, R. D. (2022). *Education is about to radically change: AI for the masses.* Getting Smart. https://www.gettingsmart.com/2022/12/16/education-is-about-to-radically-change-ai-for-the-masses/

McLeod, S. (2014). *Instead of an AUP, how about an EUP?* Dangerously Irrelevant. https://dangerouslyirrelevant.org/2014/03/instead-of-an-aup-how-about-an-eup-empowered-use-policy.html

Miller, M. (2022). *ChatGPT, chatbots and artificial intelligence in education.* Ditch That Textbook. https://ditchthattextbook.com/ai/#t-1671292150944

Momentous Institute. (2019). *Can a teacher get some help here?* https://momentousinstitute.org/resources/can-a-teacher-get-some-help-here

Myung, J., & Martinez, K. (2013). *Strategies for enhancing the impact of post-observation feedback for teachers.* Carnegie Foundation. https://www.carnegiefoundation.org/resources/publications/strategies-enhancing-impact-post-observation-feedback-teachers/

Open AI. (n.d.). *DALL•E 2.* https://openai.com/dall-e-2

OpenAI. (2020). *Introducing ChatGPT: A powerful tool for natural language generation.* OpenAI Blog. https://openai.com/blog/chatgpt/

OpenAI. (2021). *DALL•E.* https://openai.com/dall-e/

OpenAI. (2023). *Educator considerations for ChatGPT.* https://platform.openai.com/docs/chatgpt-education

OpenAI. (2023). *GPT-4 is OpenAI's most advanced system, producing safer and more useful responses.* https://openai.com/product/gpt-4

Osman, N. (2022). *AI- Automating the mundane and elevating the humane.* LinkedIn Pulse. https://www.linkedin.com/pulse/ai-automating-mundane-elevating-humane-nora-osman/

Pasick, A. (2023). Artificial intelligence glossary: Neural networks and other terms explained. *The New York Times.* https://www.nytimes.com/article/ai-artificial-intelligence-glossary.html

Perlow, S. (2023). How AI is changing writing. *The Washington Post.* https://www.washingtonpost.com/books/2023/02/13/ai-in-poetry/

Rogers-Whitehead, C. & Monterosa, V. (2023). *Deepening digital citizenship: A guide to systemwide policy and practice.* ISTE.

Ribble, M. and Park, M. (2019). *The digital citizenship handbook for school leaders: Fostering positive interactions online.* ISTE.

Sabbatini, W. (2017). How Google took over the classroom. *The New York Times.* https://www.nytimes.com/2017/05/13/technology/google-education-chromebooks-schools.html

Sevilla et al., (2022). *Compute trends across three eras of machine learning* [Conference presentation abstract]. International Joint Conference on Neural Networks (IJCNN), Padua, Italy. https://arxiv.org/abs/2202.05924

Shah, P. (2023). *AI and the future of education: Teaching in the age of artificial intelligence.* Jossey-Bass.

Steindl-Rast, D. (2013). *Want to be happy? Be grateful* [Video transcript]. TED Conferences. https://www.ted.com/talks/david_steindl_rast_want_to_be_happy_be_grateful/transcript

Toner, H. (2023). *What are generative AI, large language models, and foundation models?* Center for Security and Emerging Technology. Georgetown University. https://cset.georgetown.edu/article/what-are-generative-ai-large-language-models-and-foundation-models

ua-data7. (n.d.). *AI tools landscape.* GitHub. https://github.com/ua-data7/LearningResources/wiki/AI-Tools-Landscape

U.S. Department of Education, Office of Educational Technology (2023). *Artificial intelligence and future of teaching and learning: Insights and recommendations.* https://www2.ed.gov/documents/ai-report/ai-report.pdf

Verma, P., & Oremus, W. (2023). What happens when ChatGPT lies about real people? *The Washington Post.* https://www.washingtonpost.com/technology/2023/04/05/chatgpt-lies/?utm_source=cordial&utm_medium=email&utm_campaign=hp-us-reg-morning-email_2023-04-06

Vincent, J. (2022). *AI-generated imagery is the new clip art as Microsoft adds DALL-E to its Office suite.* The Verge. https://www.theverge.com/2022/10/12/23400270/ai-generated-art-dall-e-microsoft-designer-app-office-365-suite

White, M. J. (2023). *ChatGPT 4: everything we know so far.* Digital Trends. https://www.digitaltrends.com/computing/chatgpt-4-everything-we-know-so-far/

INDEX

www.ingramcontent.com/pod-product-compliance
Lightning Source LLC
LaVergne TN
LVHW081342050326
832903LV00024B/1272